1001 COOL INVENTIONS

with Glen Singleton

HINKLER BOOKS

Author: Ben Ripley
Illustrator: Glen Singleton
Cover Design: Hinkler Books Design Studio
Typesetter: Midland Typesetters

1001 Cool Inventions
Published in 2006 by Hinkler Books Pty Ltd
45–55 Fairchild Street
Heatherton VIC 3202 Australia
www.hinklerbooks.com

15 14 13 12 11 10 9 8 7
12 11 10

ISBN: 978 1 7415 7504 0
Printed and bound in China

CONTENTS

Introduction

We live in a world full of wonder. Most of the time we take the things around us for granted, but every now and again our curiosity leads us to ask questions about their origin.

Human beings are unlike any other creature on the planet because of our ability to think, invent and progress beyond our imagination. Where would we be now if someone had not thought of the idea of the wheel, the loom or the Ninja Turtle?

This book is divided up into different sections and covers the earliest inventions in history to the wonders of modern science. Also included are some magnificent inventions of the imagination and a section on some of the latest invented buzzwords that have entered our language over the past few years.

There is something in here for everyone, and who knows, this book may inspire you to be the next great inventor of the twenty-first century!

Gronk tries to decide
whether to invent
the jet engine,
the telephone,
the electric lightbulb
or the toothpaste tube...

but finally settles
on the
NUTCRACKER

Early Days

UGGH thought the piece of stick with a sharp rock tied to the end was just a stick with a sharp rock tied to the end...
Then he realised just what it could do.

Oh my! I think I've invented the AXE!

1 **T**ools have been around for three million years! Early people used sharpened stones to cut things up, or to chop wood.

2 **T**he first axe may have taken another million years to perfect. This was done simply by sharpening a stone to a thin blade.

3 **A** few thousand years later, an axe with a heavy base and a longer, straighter edge would be used.

4 **F**ire has been around for ever! It was easy enough to keep a fire going once it started naturally but it was a while before people realised they could make fire themselves, through friction caused by two sticks being rubbed together.

Ahhrr! Look at that! I've wrecked a perfectly good drill. It's gone and caught fire! I'd better put it out!

Grunt, the slowest Neanderthal of the cave, doesn't see the potential of his burning drill.

5 **T**he act of rolling a stick between the palms of one's hands may also have sparked the idea of a drill as well as fire. A spinning stick could easily burrow its way into the ground.

6 **S**harp stones were not only used as weapons. They were also adapted to use as designing tools to carve intricate details on other objects.

7 **C**ro-Magnon people perfected the art of fishing by using small bones, sharpened with tools tied to plant vines. The 'hook' would lodge in the fish's throat, like a modern steel hook.

8 **D**ifferent types of tools were experimented with and one, with a sharpened tip rather than a side blade, was to become the chisel.

9 **L**onger sharpened tools made from wood were used for cutting down crops. Later, people worked out that if the blade was curved it would be more time-efficient because it could cut down more crops with each swing.

10 **W**e know that the bow and arrow as a combined weapon has been around for over 30 000 years because it is depicted in cave paintings.

11 **T**he crossbow would come much later. It was invented around 2500 years ago. The first was called a gastrophetes, so named because it was held against the stomach when fired!

12 Ancient cave paintings have provided endless theories as to what they depict, and also what they were painted with. It has been suggested that the first paintbrush was merely a stick that had been chewed at the end until the fibres feathered out into a brush.

13 Early people were resourceful and used much of their surroundings to make useful tools. Plants often proved invaluable, for example by binding lengths of various vines, the first type of rope was made.

14 People lived in caves for thousands of years but eventually they began to build shelters out of anything they could find, particularly rock, bones and mud.

15 It was only just over 7000 years ago that people made bricks out of hardened mud with bundled straw inside to strengthen them. It would be another 2000 years before bricks were being baked in a kiln.

16 Around 20 000 years ago, people threw sticks at animals in order to kill them. Eventually, it was realised that shapes flew faster and possibly returned to the thrower. This was the first boomerang.

17 The sling is also a very early weapon. It was a simple strap of leather folded double with a stone to hurl held in the fold. Then with a forceful swing, the item was projected through the air.

18 The sling was a useful tool but had its limitations. However, it wasn't until around 400 BC that the catapult was invented. It had far more power and threw much heavier objects – even though they didn't always hit their desired target.

19 Thanks to witnessing the effect the hot sun had on mud, people realised they could create useful pottery objects by heating moulded mud in a fire.

20 It may have taken another 5000 years before it was realised that it was more productive and energy-efficient to make a fire under a built furnace and cook food inside it. This discovery would lead to the first oven!

21 One of the most ingenious early inventions was the loom, around 5000 BC. People realised it was possible to weave fibres to make cloth. The loom helped the weaver by separating alternate warp threads so the needle (or 'weft') could pass through them.

22 The wheel revolutionised the world. However, it is suggested that the first wheels were not built for transportation but for rotating clay when making pottery!

After an unexpected mishap in the workshop, Thurk loses control of his potter's wheel. Closing his potter's business the same afternoon, he re-opens the next morning selling his new invention... WHEELS!

23 The idea of rotation helped with the development of other tools, including the lathe, which cut in a circular pattern when an object was rotated against the blade.

24 Around the same time, the lever was putting simple physics into practice. By using an object as a pivot, a heavy item could be moved with less force than before.

25 Around 3400 BC, people counted just by making marks in a row. However, the ancient Egyptians came up with the idea of using different-shaped marks to symbolise ones, tens and hundreds!

26 Writing wasn't far off; just another 300 years later the Sumerians were marking symbols down in clay in order to keep track of their businesses. Historians have named this early form of writing cuneiform.

27 **C**andles were first used around 5000 years ago and they haven't changed much since. The wick was dipped repeatedly in melted bees-wax until it built up to a thick coating.

28 **E**gyptians were always far ahead of their time. In 3000 BC they were using cosmetics on their skin, including moisturiser. Often paints were used to beautify or, in some cases, terrify!

29 **T**he calendar has had its fair share of alterations. Five thousand years ago the Babylonians had a calendar based on the movement of the sun and moon. However, the Egyptians were aware of how inaccurate this could be, so relied only on the sun.

30 **I**t was the Babylonians who devised the sixty seconds in a minute and sixty minutes in an hour calculation that we use to this day.

31 **T**he Babylonians went on to improve the calendar system once more, thanks to their astronomers, who figured out the cycles of the moon and stars. It took a few alterations but eventually, around 380 BC, their calendar stabilised – for a while, at least.

32 It wasn't until 45 BC that Julius Caesar decided to create a new calendar based on a 365-day year. He even called it the Julian calendar, after himself!

33 Pope Gregory XIII invented the Gregorian calendar in 1582. This new calendar was based on Julius Caesar's but he omitted a few days so the seasons always fell into place. We still use this perfected form today.

34 The ancient Egyptians were not the sort of people to let things get in the way of progress. When the city of Memphis was under threat of flooding from the rising Nile, they built what is likely to have been the very first dam.

What's this? It looks like water! Go quickly, Hamadi! Go build a dam across the Nile. And make it snappy!

King Cheops appoints his first Minister for Dams when he finds the palace half full of water.

35 Ancient Egyptians were also the inventors of the forerunner of paper, papyrus. They flattened reeds until they became bound together. Then they polished the sheets with stones to make them even flatter and smoother for writing on.

36 The ink used by ancient Egyptians to write on papyrus was a combination of glue and soot. It was initially dry, so it had to be moistened before use.

After only ten minutes into his job as royal scribe, Akhenaten realised that dry papyrus ink and a black tongue were not for him... So decided his old day job dragging rocks around the pyramids was not so bad after all.

37 Later on, around 2400 BC, a form of leather that was treated to be paler than most was used to write upon. This was to become known as parchment.

38 The heating of sand with limestone produces glass, and for many years glass was used mainly for ornamental purposes. The ancient Egyptians would eventually work with it. They began to make glass containers 3500 years ago.

39 It wasn't until 1300 AD that glass mirrors were made by the Venetians. Before that, shiny metals such as silver and bronze were the main reflective surfaces used by vain people!

40 It has been suggested that the ancient Egyptians were the first people to invent tongs, most likely as a way to hold their glass creations in the fire as they heated them.

41 As time moved on, people began to develop a sense of hygiene. Eventually, the concept of separate areas for washing began to take shape. Approximately 4000 years ago, people in India built homes with drainage systems to carry waste away from living areas.

While Zakros tumbles from the wall of the Temple of the Raging Bull and is caught in an overgrown potato creeper, one of his friends sees potential in the bad situation.

Hey! Stick a seat on that vine, Zakros, and that would make a great swing!

42 **R**unning water was a surprisingly late invention, even though there had been bathrooms in India. It was the royalty of Crete at the palace of King Minos who had the first pipe system installed around 1700 BC.

43 **T**he Minoans of Crete were also the first to fully develop the concept of the swing, from just swinging on a vine or creeper to placing an actual seat on the looped end.

44 **F**lags were invented by the Chinese around 1500 BC. They were significant to the owner, but were even more so to the enemy of the owner. The flag captured during battle, would signify defeat!

Carry the flag for five minutes would you me old chum...just to give my arms a rest.

No way matey! They always shoot the guy who's carrying the flag!

45 **A**lthough the Greeks invented metal body armour in 800 BC, the Chinese were making their own 300 years earlier out of the skin of the rhinoceros, which is incredibly thick and strong.

46 **C**hain mail was a way of making armour lighter and easier to move in and was invented by the Greeks in 200 BC.

47 The Greeks discovered the first magnetic rock around 3000 years ago in a place called Magnesia, which gave the mineral its name.

48 Oil has been used for burning and providing a light source for thousands of years. Around 700 BC, the Greeks created lamps with wicks sitting in a pool of oil. The Chinese and Egyptians used similar lamps even earlier.

49 The Egyptians were also the pioneers of the sundial, or certainly a distant relative of one – the shadow clock. The sun would cast a shadow and, depending on where the shadow was on a scale of marked hours, one could tell the time of day.

50 The first waterwheel was used by the Greeks in a corn mill just over 2000 years ago. This was so successful that it wasn't long before the Romans made larger models. Water wheels are still in use today.

51 The abacus may have been invented around 2400 BC by the Babylonians but we do know it was also used by the Chinese and the Romans.

Domestic Life

52 The first chairs of a design we are familiar with today may well be nearly 5000 years old. Carved seats and thrones have been found in the tombs of ancient Egyptian kings.

I'm the Pharaoh of all Egypt... They give me gold, jewels, precious stones, chariots, slaves and expensive carved furniture. You'd think someone could find me a soft cushion to sit on!

53 Carpets were also created by the ancient Egyptians, who wove their own.

54 Linoleum, however, was a much later invention. In 1861, Frederick Walton, a British rubber manufacturer wanted to make a smooth, washable floor surface. He worked to create a substance made from linseed oils and other materials, and invented linoleum (or lino). It is still used today.

Could someone pass the side of pig and the wooden bowl of gruel. Where's the pig? I can't even see the table! That's not the gruel. That's the wash bucket! Where's my chair? Hey! That's my leg! Get your hands off my jug of ale! How do you know it's my hand? I can't even see my hand.

It's dinner time on the 1st January 1100... the night before somebody invented the chimney.

55 Since fire was discovered, there has always been a need to guide the smoke that comes from it. It wasn't until the beginning of the twelfth century in Europe that people invented a chimney (rather than just a hole in the roof) that would draw the smoke through a flue and out of buildings.

56 **A**lthough James King first invented a washing machine with a drum in 1851, Alva J Fisher invented the first electric machine in 1908.

57 **T**umble dryers are the next logical step from the washing machine and they work on the same drum principle. In this case, hot air is generated and circulated around the

Oohh! Well if nothing else... it got the stains out!

James King's wife tries out her husband's new invention... The washing machine

fabrics which 'tumble' within the rotating drum. The first tumble dryer was made in 1931 by the Huebsch Manufacturing Company.

58 **H**enry Seely invented the electric iron in 1882. It wasn't until the 1950s that steam irons were developed.

59 **T**he sewing machine had many prototypes from many different inventors around the world. The first successful one was the brainchild of a Frenchman, Barthelemy Thimonier, in 1830. Sadly, a group of angry tailors ransacked his factory for fear of unemployment.

While standing just that bit too close to the radar he was working on with a pocket full of sweets... Engineer Percy Spencer accidentally invents the microwave oven ...and even more importantly... IRRADIATED TOFFEE!

60 **P**ercy Spencer invented the microwave oven in 1946. He was an engineer for the Raytheon Company in the USA, and while he was experimenting with radar, he found some sweets had melted in his pockets. This gave him the idea for the microwave oven.

61 In the early nineteenth century, showers were beginning to become popular. In 1810, an English regency shower pumped water on to the bather's head, and the 1830s American Virginia Stool Shower was a wooden chair with a lever to release water.

62 The wonderful relaxation of a whirlpool bath feels like such a naughty indulgence! The first one was invented in 1968 by Roy Jacuzzi, who gave his name to the product. His original pumps were used by farmers but he had the idea of applying them to a bathtub.

63 Sir John Harrington built the first toilet for his godmother, Queen Elizabeth of England, in 1596. He was ridiculed for the idea and never made any more. Although many inventors copied the style, it wasn't until 1885 that Thomas Twyford built the classic china bowl rather than the original wooden sort.

64 A couple of cousins named Edwin Shoemaker and Edward Knabusch designed the first recliner chair called the La-Z-Boy, which is still available today in a much-modified form.

65 In 1903 Herbert Booth became the brains behind the vacuum cleaner, although it was the Hoover that became the most famous design.

James Dyson, determined to invent a vacuum cleaner without a bag, tries just vacuuming without a bag to give it a try.

66 In 1983, James Dyson changed the way of vacuuming by introducing the cyclonic vacuum cleaner. For once, it had no bag!

67 In 1851, Dr John Gorrie came up with the idea of a refrigerator, inspired by his plan to keep fevered patients cool through pressured gas. Nearly a decade later, Ferdinand Carre would develop the idea further to make the refrigerators we are accustomed to today.

68 The notion of quick freezing food came from Clarence Birdseye in 1912. Whilst on a trip to Newfoundland, Canada, he saw that the residents left fish outside to keep fresh, as it was so cold. Clarence invented a machine that would quick freeze foodstuffs, retaining the flavour.

69 Air conditioners were the invention of Willis Carrier in 1902. He realised it was possible to control the humidity in the air through refrigeration.

What do you think of my new invention... THE CYLINDER PIN-TUMBLE LOCK?

DOES IT HAVE A KEY?

CLICK

No. But that's a good idea, young man. I'll get onto it right away!

70 There have been many variations of the lock over the past 4000 years. Many inventors have had variable success with their designs but it is the name Linus Yale Jr that goes down in history, after he invented the cylinder pin-tumble lock in 1861.

71 Levi Hutchins of New Hampshire invented the first mechanical alarm clock in 1787. The only problem was the alarm would only go off at four o'clock!

72 Englishman George Darby invented the first heat detector in 1902. This device would sound an alarm if the temperature reached a certain degree. In 1976, Sidney Jacoby invented an improved system.

73 The smoke alarm is based on a similar principle and one designed by BRK Electronics in 1967 detected the smoke particles and set off a shrieking noise.

74 Harry and Mary Jackson were pioneers in protective security. In the 1930s, they invented the modern burglar alarm.

75 Marie Brown patented the first video security system in 1969, which used video surveillance to see who was at your front door.

76 **S**ecurity screens are becoming more and more commonplace. John Golding of Chicago first developed these in 1884.

77 **S**cales have been around in one form or another for nearly 6000 years. Kitchen weighing scales have come in many different forms and no specific inventor is known.

78 **C**at litter was thought of by Edward Lowe in the 1940s. Beforehand, sand was often the option for the indoor cat. Hearing a neighbour complain about the messy sand, Lowe came up with the idea of using absorbent clay.

79 **S**oap was not always used for washing. For many years a soap-like mixture of fat and ash was used for medicinal purposes, but in the second century the Romans made a similar compound to clean items and themselves.

80 **T**he thermostats that are in use today have a history that dates back to approximately 1600, when a Dutchman named Cornelius Drebbel combined the thermometer with a damper in a furnace.

81 Denis Papin invented the pressure cooker in 1679. He designed a pan with a reservoir inside it which could be heated to raise the pressure. A valve on top prevented the water from boiling over.

82 Light bulbs wouldn't exist in their current form if it were not for the discovery of tungsten. Tungsten is the material within the bulb that heats up and glows brightly. Two brothers from Spain, Fausto and Juan D'Elhuyar, were the first to discover this ingenious way of producing light with tungsten in 1783.

Life at midnight before the light bulb was invented. Life at midnight after the lightbulb was invented.

83 Thomas Edison and Joseph Swan both independently came up with the idea of using carbon within a light bulb to create light in the mid-1800s. By the end of the nineteenth century, light bulbs were being used in most places around the world.

84 Although seemingly dangerous, gas was for decades a very popular way of lighting the home. This is thanks to William Murdoch, a Scotsman who had relocated to Cornwall in the south of England, who lit his home by igniting the gas he produced from burning coals.

DON'T LEAN ON THAT WALL! Without cement that wall is just...

A pile of bricks!

85 Cement used for building is also known as Portland cement and was invented by Joseph Aspdin in 1824. He was a British builder, and he mixed limestone and clay to form a stronger substance.

86 In 1928, Eugene Freyssinet overcame the problem of cracking concrete by laying wire into the wet form before it set.

87 The lawnmower was a handy replacement for the grass-chewing goats and sheep. Edwin Budding designed the first one in 1830. It had a cylinder at the front with sharp blades for slicing through even the thickest patches of grass. It would be a while before someone thought to attach a bucket to catch the excess grass, though.

The word is...somebody's invented a lawnmower. We'd better eat grass faster...and lay off nibbling the hedges!

88 The 'prefab' is a building made up of prefabricated parts ready to construct. Similar to a kit, the parts can easily be erected following a basic plan. Crystal Palace in London was a spectacular prefab exhibition hall made of glass and iron. Designed by Joseph Paxton in 1851, it took six months to put together.

89 The can-opener was invented by Robert Yeates in 1855. It was a simple sharp blade that was jammed into the top of the can and moved around the rim. Before that, cans were opened using a hammer and chisel.

WHY RING PU CANS WERE INVENTED.

SHAKE SHAKE

90 The ring-pull (initially on drink cans, but eventually stronger versions on food tins) was invented by Ermal Fraze in 1966.

91 In 1976, the safer and stronger ring pull was invented by American Daniel Cudzic because too many people were cutting themselves on the old style.

92 Fibreglass is often used for insulation in modern homes. It was invented by Russell Games Slayter in 1938 and is made from extremely fine glass fibres.

93 The skyscraper is a tall building with a steel frame, and the first one was merely ten storeys high. It was built in Chicago in the USA in 1885 and was designed by William Jenney.

94 The safety razor was a welcome replacement for the sharp knife-like blade that was used for shaving until King C. Gillette introduced the disposable razor in 1901.

95 The first electric razor was invented in 1928 by Jacob Schick, whose name is still known today on shaving products.

96 Stainless steel was invented in Sheffield, England, in 1913. It was thirteen per cent chromium and was tough enough to withstand corrosion. This invention was first used for cutlery.

97 It wasn't possible to be woken up with a nice cup of tea without having your own personal staff until Frank Clarke invented the very first 'teas maid' in 1902. This was a combination alarm clock and tea maker. At a certain time, a match would automatically be struck to light a flame beneath a kettle of water. Steam caused the kettle to tip into the teapot. Thankfully, this clumsy invention has been refined a great deal over the years!

98 The comforting nature of a teddy bear is hard to explain, but its history is simpler. After US president Theodore Roosevelt couldn't bring himself to kill a bear cub on a shooting trip, a retailer named Morris Mitchtom created toy bears for children and named them after the shortened form of Theodore; Teddy. A German women named Margarete Steiff made similar toys that went on to become the more famous design.

99 Herbert Johnson designed a food mixer for domestic purposes in 1919. The bowl rotated in one direction and the beaters turned in the other.

100 The food processor did a lot more than the basic mixer. It could also dice and shred foods into tiny pieces. The first one was invented by Frenchman Pierre Verdon in 1971.

101 John Rawlings was the man behind the rawlplug. This little plug is a neat and convenient way of attaching things via screws to the wall of the home.

102 Cotton buds or Q-tips® were invented by a Polish man named Leo Gerstenzang in 1925, but credit goes to his wife, who gave him the idea when he saw her cleaning her baby with cotton wool and toothpicks.

103 The aerosol spray can was a Norwegian invention. In 1926, Erik Rothheim used the idea for spray paint. Spray cans were also used later by Lyle Goodhue in the USA for spraying insecticide on bugs.

104 Charles Strite was the inventor of the pop-up toaster in 1919. Originally it was designed for catering kitchens. The household version didn't reach the market until 1926.

105 Chemicals like ammonia were used inside the first electric refrigerators, but they proved to be poisonous to humans. In 1928, Thomas Midgley Jr and Albert Henne came up with chlorofluorocarbons (CFCs), which seemed to do the trick. However, they didn't realise the damage CFCs were doing to the Earth's atmosphere. Chlorofluorocarbons were banned from the 1990s onwards.

106 'The best thing since sliced bread!' Well, what did they say before sliced bread? Otto Rohwedder invented the first machine to slice and package bread in 1928 in the USA. Soon it became incredibly popular. No more doorstop slices!

OTTO ROHWEDDER GETS THE IDEA FOR A BREAD SLICING MACHINE....JUST BEFORE HE HITS THE FLOOR.

107 Sticky tape was invented by the Minnesota Mining and Manufacturing Company (also known as 3M) in 1925 and was an answer to how to seal the wrapping of cellophane around products.

108 Superglue® is a glue which, in reaction to a surface with water in it, turns into a stiff plastic. It was invented in 1958 by Harry Coover and Fred Joyner. But beware, your body is full of water and it will stick to your skin!

109 Cling film, Saran Wrap® or Gladwrap® was an invention of the Dow Chemical Company. It was invented in 1933 and fully marketed in 1949.

110 Teflon® is a product used in various ways but most commonly on pans to make them non-stick. It was discovered by accident by Roy Plunkett in 1938.

111 The glass used for windows is not just ordinary glass. It is called 'float glass'. Float glass is made by pouring molten glass onto molten tin. Heat is used to smooth the surfaces. This process was invented in 1952, but it wasn't until 1959 that it was put into practice commercially.

112 In 2001, Kevin Sanderson from Pilkington's Glass Company in Britain invented a coating that, when placed on windows, makes them self-cleaning. The coating contains an agent that enables oxygen and light to unstick any dirt that may be caught in it. The rain can wash any excess away.

Jean looks out of her filthy mucky dirty SELF CLEANING WINDOWS to greet the new day with full confidence her windows will clean themselves with the next shower of rain.

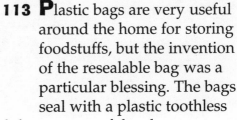

Steve Ausnit from Romania gives away his idea of a ZIPPER LOCK BAG after getting his beard and an awful floral tie badly caught in the zipper teeth.

113 Plastic bags are very useful around the home for storing foodstuffs, but the invention of the resealable bag was a particular blessing. The bags seal with a plastic toothless zip action. They had three stages of development, firstly by Danish Borgda Madsen in the 1940s, then by Steve Ausnit from Romania in the 1950s, and then finally a Japanese inventor called Kakuji Naito made the perfectly airtight form.

114 Step out of the home into many people's garages and you just might see a Workmate® bench. This multipurpose tool was invented by Ron Hickman in 1968. In 1972, the famous company Black and Decker began full production of the basic Workmate® and has since sold millions.

Neil Arnott in 1873 tries out his new invention the Waterbed in full military costume. Unfortunately he dreams of the Battle of Waterloo sometime during the night...

Swim fer yer lives me hearties!

115 The waterbed was designed by Neil Arnott in 1873 and was intended as a cure for bedsores.

116 The first swivel chair was invented in the late 1700s by none other than the third President of the United States, Thomas Jefferson.

117 A New Orleans inventor named John Hampson patented adjustable Venetian blinds in 1841.

118 The rotary washing line, known as the Hills Hoist®, was invented by Australian Lance Hill in 1945. Not only does his washing line rotate, it also has a handle to lower and raise the line, to make hanging out the washing easier.

Do you know what country the ROTARY WASHING LINE was invented in?

No. Search me!

119 In 2004, a twenty-seven-year-old Hungarian inventor named Aron Losonczi made a new type of concrete with optical fibres inside it, so it could emit light.

120 Blu-tack® is a putty-like substance used for sticking posters to walls. The name is trademarked to the Australian Bostik Findley Company and it went on sale in 1971.

121 Electric blankets have existed in one form or another since the early 1900s. The first automatic electric blanket was made in 1936 and it had its own thermostat, which helped it maintain a reasonable temperature.

122 There are conflicting reports as to who invented the lava-lamp. One theory holds that Englishman Richard Torti invented it in the 1960s and he eventually sold his idea to the Mathmos Company. The other theory claims it was an inventor named Craven Walker.

123 The aquarium is first recorded in history when English diarist Samuel Pepys noted seeing fish being displayed in a glass tank in London, in 1665.

124 The cat flap is one of Isaac Newton's lesser-known inventions, but all the same, he devised the mini door for the cat back in the seventeenth century!

125 In New York City in 1882, the first tree to be adorned with electric lights was lit by Edward Johnson. He would go on to produce the first string of Christmas lights, or fairy lights, as they are commonly known.

Keeping in Touch

126 **A**lthough people were able to communicate through speech and, for a long time, through the aid of pictures, it wasn't until around 3000 years ago that the first written languages appeared. The Greeks adapted a system from the Palestinians using patterns of consonants and vowels. This was a distant relative of the alphabet we know today.

127 **H**ieroglyphics are a form of writing developed by the ancient Egyptians (although not exclusively). Pictures were used to represent words, letters and concepts. A quail chick, an owl, a reed and a vulture are just a few of the symbols to represent letters.

What can you see through your telescope, Corporal?

I can see a Frenchman standing on a grassy hilltop doing what looks like some sort of folk dance with flags Sir!

The first semaphore message works perfectly, completely confusing the enemy.

128 **M**ost people know semaphore as the communication of letters through different positions of hand-held flags, but the original semaphore was a signalling system invented by the Chappe Brothers of France in 1792. It was used to pass information between France and Austria.

129 **S**moke signalling is an ancient form of communication used by both the Native Americans and the Chinese. By fanning the smoke of a fire with a blanket, different clouds can be formed to mean different things.

So he's saying... White man coming in large numbers? Then what does he say?

He says... My smoke signal blanket catch on fire.

130 There are many Creole and pidgin languages (languages that develop from a mixture of two languages) in the world that enable people of different language backgrounds to communicate. The most successful attempt to create a universal language is Esperanto. Ludwik Zamenhof invented it in 1887 and it is based on a variety of European languages.

131 Sign language was not the invention of one person. It came into existence through necessity, as people who were deaf had to find a way to communicate. Just as there are different spoken languages, there are also different sign languages.

132 Chinese whispers is a game where players pass on a sentence by whispering it to another player. It is passed on again, until after a number of repetitions the information is shared, usually much altered. A story about its origins tells how an officer sent the message 'Send reinforcements, we're going to advance' along a relay of soldiers, only for it to reach the intended recipient as 'Send three and four pence, we're going to a dance'!

133 Louis Braille was blinded at the age of three and by the time he was fifteen he had invented the system to assist blind people that was named after him. Each letter of the alphabet is represented by a sequence of dots within a cell of six. The raised dots can be read by running a finger over them and recognising the pattern.

134 **W**hich newspaper came first? The *Relation* or the *Avisa Relation oder Zeitung*? No one knows for sure. Both were started in Germany in 1609 but by the middle of the seventeenth century, newspapers were popular all over Europe.

135 **P**encils were an idea of Conrad Gesner from Germany, who took the soft material of carbon and encased it in wood in 1565.

136 **A**round 2500 years ago, ancient Greeks used pens that were made of wood. The wood was sharpened to a point and had a groove leading down to the tip through which ink could flow.

137 **F**ountain pens were originally called 'reservoir pens' because ink was held in the body of the pen rather than the writer having to dip the end into a pot. These were around as far back as the 1700s. In the 1850s fountain pens became popular and many different designs were patented. They could be filled with an eyedropper or used air pressure to suck the ink up inside the pen. Many years later, the ink cartridge became popular.

138 The feathered pen, or quill, was first used around 500 AD. It was ideal for writing as the feather was hollow and could hold ink, and the tip

A goose leaving town really fast after discovering goose feathers were becoming very popular as quills for writing.

could be sharpened to a fine point. Goose feathers were the most popular.

Oh you've got one of those new ballpoint pens!

How do you know?

I can see it's leaking in your pocket.

139 The ballpoint pen was invented in 1938. It was the brainchild of Hungarian brothers Ladislao and Georg Biro.

140 The very first postage stamp was made in Great Britain in 1840. It was called the Penny Black and it had a picture of Queen Victoria's head on it. It was invented by Rowland Hill and it was adhesive, enabling it to be stuck to an envelope. Hill was knighted for his work.

141 One of the first postal services was in 1653, in France. A maker of envelopes called De Valayer offered to deliver any mail placed into the mail boxes he provided, but only on the condition that his envelopes were used.

142 A painter from England named John Horsley was commissioned to design the very first Christmas card. Londoners were able to purchase it in 1843.

143 The typewriter has no single inventor, as many people contributed ideas toward a machine that could write. William Austin Burt made a typographer in 1829 and Pellegrino Turri invented carbon paper but an Austrian named Peter Mitterhofer designed the typewriter that we would most easily recognise today.

144 The QWERTY keyboard which is now standard was designed and patented by Christopher Sholes in 1868. It made typing easier by not placing too many common pairs of letters together and enabled two-hand typing to flow without the constant need to unblock the typewriter's lettered arms. It is interesting to note that the word 'typewriter' can be typed out easily across the top row of letters!

145 In 1874, three men from America named Christopher Sholes, Carlos Glidden and Samuel Soule invented a typewriter that was faster and more efficient than Mitterhofer's. However, it only typed in capital letters!

146 Seymour Rubenstein from America developed WordStar, the first popular word processor software package for personal computers. Developed in 1979, it was eagerly received in the marketplace.

147 Morse code was the invention of Samuel Morse in 1832. Morse came up with the idea of an electromagnetic telegraph system while talking to a colleague,

and then proceeded to jot down the dot-dash system into his notebook. However, he didn't apply for the patent until 1837.

148 The telephone was invented by Alexander Graham Bell, who was in competition with rival inventor, Elisha Gray. On 10 March in 1876, Bell succeeded with his creation and by 1877 he had begun his own telephone company.

149 David Hughes invented the printing telegraph in 1855. The first machines using Morse code seemed a little complicated so he made a machine that could send written messages and have them printed out at the other end.

150 The first telegraph cable to stretch across the Atlantic was laid in 1858 by a group of scientists. Although the first line failed after a few weeks, it paved the way for future successful attempts.

SHAMUS O'MALLEY DISCOVERS THE FIRST TRANSATLANTIC CABLE OFF THE COAST OF IRELAND.

151 In 1892, the combined efforts of Oliver Heaviside and physicist Michael Pupin helped to improve long distance cabling for telephone wires through the addition of recurring coils along the line.

152 Ethernet, the standard for connecting computers in a Local Area Network (LAN), was first developed by Robert Metcalfe in the early 1970s. It allowed computers to communicate over a shared cable without interrupting each others' transmissions.

153 Fax is short for facsimile. A fax is a machine that can send and receive printed information through wires. It was developed in 1843 by a Scottish inventor and clockmaker named Alexander Bain but the design wasn't improved until Samuel Morse invented the telegraph. In its early life, the fax interpreted signals and printed them out on paper. It would be a long time before replicas of documents could be sent and received.

Is thart tha wee FAX MACHINE we've been hearin about Mr Bain? Or is thart a clork?

Arrch nor Mrs Brown. Thart's Tiddles the wee cart!

Alexander Bain a clockmaker, develops the first fax machine.

I'm sorry... I can't hear you. I'm losing my signal. Just wait while I drag my mobile phone to a different spot.

The early MOBILE PHONE

154 Today, just about everyone who is old enough owns a mobile or cellular phone, and it is hard to think of life without one. It all started back in 1979 in the Bell Telephone Laboratories in the USA. It took many years for mobile phones to reduce in size and become readily available to the public.

155 The digital mobile phone was the successor to the analogue phone and was designed in 1982 by the 'Groupe Special Mobile' in Europe. The perfected system was up and running by 1991.

156 The modern satellite mobile phone was instituted in 1998 and used sixty-six satellites orbiting Earth. Satellite phones have been in use since 1982, but the newer ones from the Iridium Mobile Network are clearer due to the lower orbits of the satellites.

157 There were prototype answering machines as early as 1898. The telegraphone used magnetic recording technology which could retain messages on a reel.

158 Answering machines have come in several different forms. In 1960, Japanese inventor Dr Kazuo Hashimoto created the Ansaphone®, which was the first to be sold in the USA. In 1971 Casio created the Model 400 which could hold up to twenty messages.

159 Voicemail is a much more advanced system and is very popular today on mobile phones in particular. Voicemail was invented by Gordon Matthews in 1983.

160 **W**alkie-talkies were invented by Canadian Al Gross in 1938, which led to the systems used by the police force and taxi drivers. He went on to pioneer CB (Citizens' Band) radio in 1948. Although walkie-talkiesare generally for official use, toy models have been incredibly popular with children.

161 **T**he modem is for sending and receiving data over telephone lines and decoding digital information. Its name is derived from the term modulator/demodulator. Modems were first sold commerically by AT&T in 1962.

162 **T**he mobile phone can also access the Internet but not without the wireless application protocol that was invented in 1997.

163 **F**or many years, people had to 'dial' a telephone number, which involved rotating a numbered disc for each number. Push-button phones were invented in 1963 by the company AT&T, and were much easier on everyone's wrists.

164 **A**T&T also invented the electronic telephone exchange, although the system was partly mechanical in order to adapt to the older system easily. It was introduced in 1965.

165 The pager, often used by doctors, also had a short lifespan with the general public before mobile phones took over our lives. A Canadian named Al Gross, who also invented the walkie-talkie, developed the pager system for a hospital in New York in 1949.

BEEP BEEP BEEP BEEP BEEP BEEP

WHAT'S THAT? OH... IT MUST BE MY PAGER!

DESPITE PUBLIC NOTICES ON THE WAY INTO THE MOVIES ABOUT TURNING OFF MOBILE PHONES, DOCTOR BOB OVERLOOKS TURNING OFF HIS PAGER

166 Radio has a complex history but the names most people remember as having a part in its invention are Guglielmo Marconi and Nikola Tesla, who discovered how to transmit data over a wireless connection using the electromagnetic wave spectrum.

167 The Post-It® note owes its existence to Dr Spencer Silver, who worked for the 3M company. In 1968 he invented the adhesive backing that sticks but leaves no residue when the object is removed. In 1974 his colleague Arthur Fry used the adhesive on a bookmark for his hymn book. Seeing their workers' interest in the product, 3M launched the Post-It in the early 80s.

Now I've stuck one of those Post-it notes to remind me about something...but I can't remember what it is...or where I put the note.

168 The notepad was an Australian invention, although not the idea of a wad of paper, which had been around for years. J.A. Burchall was the person who stacked the paper on a cardboard backing and glued one edge!

169 The word Dictaphone® is actually a trademarked name but it has become custom to call all such equipment by that name. Originally, Dictaphones® were bulky machines with a funnel into which you spoke and the sound was recorded onto a phonograph cylinder. After the invention of magnetic tape, the devices became much smaller and could be hand-held.

Hi y'all everybardy! Just sit yerselves back and reelax and jest listen to ma golden tonsils wobblin'. I know yer really wantin' to hear ma geetar too... So y'all listen in, folks!

WHY DID ANYONE INVENT THE MICROPHONE?

170 The first microphone was invented by Emile Berliner in 1877 but the first practical design was invented by Alexander Graham Bell. Berliner would eventually work for the Bell Company until 1883.

171 The megaphone is a device capable of making the human voice much louder. The first megaphones were worn by actors. They wore masks made with funnelled mouths in order to help the audience to hear speech better. Nowadays, megaphones are most often connected with irate movie directors and Cecil B. DeMille was apparently the first major film director to use one on set.

ROMEO...ROMEO... WHEREFORE ART THOU ROMEO?

I don't blame Romeo for not turning up... I wouldn't want a woman screaming at me through a megaphone.

172 Hearing aids were once large funnels held up to a deaf person's ear and were known as 'ear-trumpets'. The electronic hearing aid was invented by various people. Depending on the size of the battery, the devices are practically invisible when worn in the ear.

Let Me Entertain You!

173 In 1050, a monk named Guido of Arezzo began writing music down in various forms in order to make a record rather than relying on people's memories of tunes. He began with five lines to make a stave and placed marks on it to indicate the different notes. It would take 500 years to perfect this system, but Guido would be recognised as the brains behind it.

174 Around 1525, a French printer named Pierre Attaignant perfected a system where the music staves and notes could be printed at the same time. Previously these had to be printed separately. This meant music could be mass produced.

175 The first harps were used around 5000 years ago and have been linked to Egypt and Samaria. These early instruments were curved sticks with strings strung from end to end with various tensions.

176 The lyre was similar to the harp. This ancient instrument also had strings but they were stretched over the frame of a bowl or a box.

177 Another very early instrument was the bell, which 4000 years ago would be hung from a frame and then be struck by small hammers during religious events.

A one... and a two and a three... Hit it, Achenaten!

FROM A SELL OUT SEASON AT THE SPHINX
THE KING TUT QUARTET Live at The Tomb

178 **A**n early form of trumpet is actually the Australian didgeridoo. Rams' horns were also used in a similar way in the Middle East. It was the ancient Egyptians, however, who made the first metal trumpet, out of silver.

179 **Y**ou may not know what a 'sackbut' is, but it was invented around 1450 and was a musical instrument made of tubes which could be varied in length for different sounds. You may know it by its modern name – the trombone!

180 **T**he flute is just over 2000 years old, although there were simpler forms of pipe for thousands of years. The instrument we are familiar with today has its origins in China. It is a hollow pipe with finger holes, and a reed which vibrates when blown into.

2000 years ago in China while Wong was building a duck pen, he accidentally picked up a stick of bamboo, drilled holes in it and put it in his mouth and invented the flute... The ducks just ran away.

181 **T**he clarinet was invented around the turn of the eighteenth century by a German man named Johann Denner, who adapted an older instrument called the chalumeau.

182 **B**artolomeo Cristofori designed the piano in 1698, although the final perfected model was not finished until 1720. It was based on a harpsichord design but was more complex, with a much more resonant sound.

183 Ctesibius of Alexandria invented the pipe organ around 250 BC. Through combining pipes, air and water pressure and a keyboard, he created what he named the 'hydraulis', which was the forerunner of pipe organs of today.

184 The automatic piano machine was invented midway through the sixteenth century. Inside it was a cylinder with various sharp pins attached to it. As it rotated, the pins struck different notes on a keyboard and played the tune 'automatically'.

185 The very first drum was played around 8000 years ago. It was a simple instrument made from the hide of an animal stretched over a hollow object and strapped tightly down.

Gee! Thanks Dad! My very own drum kit with two sticks! And I promise I'll practise a long way from the village!

186 Thomas Edison made the first phonograph to record sound in 1877. The first sound recorded on it was 'Mary Had a Little Lamb'.

On hearing Edison's first recording, a disappointed Frank decides to return it to the store he bought it from.

Mary Had a Little Lamb...

Oh! Is that it? I was hoping to have something to dance to.

187 Swiss-born Adolf Rickenbacker moved to the USA when he was a child. He went on to create the very first electric guitar in 1932.

188 Dr Robert Moog invented the Moog synthesiser in 1963 and it became one of the most popular electronic musical instruments. This electronic keyboard revolutionised the music industry.

189 The first electronic instrument, however, was the Theremin. Invented in 1920 by Leon Theremin from Russia, it is played by moving the hands around two antennae without actually touching the instrument.

190 Leon Theremin also invented the first drum machine in 1930, called the Rhythmicon.

191 The Hammond organ was built by Laurens Hammond in the 1930s. It is similar to a regular organ, only it uses electricity to power it.

192 The accordion actually has many inventors and various designs. Among its inventors are Bernhard Eschenbach in 1810, Christian Buschmann in 1822 and Pichenot Jeune in 1831.

193 The patent for the saxophone was registered in 1846 by Adolphe Sax from Belgium. He made fourteen different types of saxophone during his lifetime.

194 One of the very first musical instruments was the whistle. It was first invented over ten thousand years ago, possibly when someone blew over a tube-shaped item such as a bone or a piece of bamboo and produced sounds.

195 The first captured motion on film was of a racehorse galloping. In 1877, the horse's owner asked British man Eadweard Muybridge to find a way of telling whether a horse's hooves were ever all off the ground at the same time. A relay of cameras along a track took pictures one after the other, and the sequence of images proved that the hooves were often all off the ground at once. This led to developments in motion picture making.

196 In 1893, William Dickson took the idea further and managed to take forty pictures a second and lay them out onto a strip of film that could be viewed through a device called a kinetoscope. These 'films' were only twenty seconds long, but did show an animated image.

197 In 1886, Chichester Bell and Charles Tainter improved the first sound recordings. At first, recordings were made on foil wrapped around a cylinder, but this was not very satisfactory and incredibly fragile. The two American inventors recorded onto wax cylinders that were more resilient and lasted for years. Their machine was called the graphophone.

198 The gramophone was invented in 1887 by Emiule Berliner and was able to play discs of recorded sound using the same principle as Bell and Tainter's graphophone. The needle was aligned in the groove on the disc, recreating the sounds and projecting them through the horn to amplify them.

199 Radio was reliant for a long time on a small piece of wire nicknamed a 'cat's whisker'. This wire lay on a crystal that detected radio waves. This development led to the transistor radio.

200 In 1906, Marconi's radio concept (see 'Keeping in Touch') was improved upon by Reginald Fessenden from Canada when he invented a generator that could produce continuous radio waves. The very first broadcast was on Christmas Eve, and people could hear music and speech.

201 Television was invented by John Logie Baird in the 1920s. By 1930, the BBC in the United Kingdom aired the first televised play, which was called *The Man with a Flower in His Mouth*.

202 Television wouldn't exist at all if it were not for the cathode ray oscilloscope. Ferdinand Braun invented it in 1897 and works it by decoding electrical messages and displaying them on a screen.

203 Colour television was standardised in the United States by the National Television Systems Committee (NTSC) in 1953, based on the work of many inventors who devised many different methods. The system was designed so that black and white televisions could still work with the new colour broadcasts.

204 Video tape recording was invented in 1951 by Charles P. Ginsberg. It was able to retain images and sound on magnetic tape that could be viewed again and again. The first VCR (video cassette recorder) wasn't available to the public until 1971.

205 **D**VDs were not the first form of disc in the revolution that replaced tapes. Laser discs were available much earlier and they were an extension of David Paul Gregg's optical disc, which he invented in 1958. DVDs (digital versatile discs) soon took over as they were a vast improvement in sound and picture quality, and they were much smaller.

206 **J**ames T. Russell from Washington in the United States developed the concept of the compact disc in the latter half of the 1960s because he was frustrated with the poor sound quality of vinyl discs and tapes.

THE EXACT MOMENT JAMES RUSSELL THOUGHT OF CREATING THE COMPACT DISC!

207 **I**t wasn't until 1980s that the two companies, Phillips and Sony, mass produced the CD format. The first CD players arrived in 1982.

208 **S**ony also created the mini disc in the early 1990s, but it failed to take off as successfully as CDs.

209 **A**pple Computer hired Tony Fadell when he approached them with the concept of the iPod, one of the first successful portable music players that can carry much more music than a cassette tape or CD.

210 **A**tari was the leading computer game manufacturer in the late seventies and early eighties. The founders were Nolan Bushnell and Ted

BOBBY SPENT MOST OF THE EARLY 70s WAITING FOR SOMEONE TO INVENT A VIDEO GAME.

Dabney, who initially made game consoles for amusement arcades. In the mid 1970s, they developed the first home video game, called 'Pong'.

211 **T**he PlayStation® was designed by the people at Sony after a project to create a super-disc with Nintendo never came to fruition. Sony developed the idea with their head engineer Ken Kutaragi.

212 **D**igital Audio Tape (DAT) was developed in the 1980s by Sony and Phillips. DAT cassettes can be used to make an exact copy of the recorded audio, unlike earlier cassettes which lost sound quality when recording.

213 **T**he computer mouse has been around since 1963 when Douglas Engelbart invented it, although back then it was a much bulkier tool.

Before developing the computer mouse as we know it, Douglas Engelbart worked on its much larger cousin, that he called... THE RAT.

214 **M**icrosoft computer software was first developed by the Microsoft Company. The company was founded in 1975 by Bill Gates and a friend. Bill Gates is now one of the world's richest men.

215 **A**pple computers were designed by Steve Jobs and Steve Wozniak with the intention of making personal computers more user-friendly.

216 **D**avid Hughes invented the carbon microphone in 1878 when he used carbon rods, a battery and an earpiece to amplify the quietest sounds. This invention would later improve the telephone.

MADGE OF LONDON COMMENTS ON HEARING THE FIRST RADIO BROADCAST IN 1920.

217 **T**he first public radio broadcasts came in 1920, in Britain. This service was started by Guglielmo Marconi. Later the same year a similar service began in the USA.

218 **F**M radio was developed in 1934 by Edwin Armstrong as a way of avoiding the interference often found on AM radio.

219 **D**isco was a music and dance craze beginning in the early 1970s, and has been heavily inspired by soul music and funk.

220 In 1979, Sony designed a portable music system that was the height of fashion during the eighties. It was named the Walkman® and played cassette tapes. However, these are now pretty much obsolete with the advent of CDs and iPods®.

221 The mini-disc player, invented in 1992, was also able to record but in the 1990s people were more interested in compact discs, which had swamped the market.

222 The jukebox has a long history. In 1889, a machine called the 'nickel-in-the-slot machine' would play music on a cylindrical phonograph when money was inserted. It was invented by Louis Glass and William Arnold.

223 Karaoke has long been part of Japanese social tradition, but the first karaoke machine was the brainwave of Daisuke Inoue in the 1970s. He pre-recorded songs for people to sing along to at parties when a 100-yen coin was inserted.

224 The Fraunhofer Institute in Germany created mp3, a system that compresses music, making it easier to download from the Internet.

225 The vinyl disc was a major milestone in playing music. In 1948, Peter Goldmark improved on it by inventing the long-playing record. It could play for twenty-five minutes on each side and was not as brittle as previous discs.

OPENING NIGHT AT THE FIRST CINEMA IN 1895.

226 Although there has been debate over who invented the first cinema, it is widely believed to be the Lumière brothers, Auguste and Louis. Their projector gave its first public performance in 1895.

227 In the 1920s, CinemaScope, the forerunner to wide-screen cinema, was invented by Frenchman Henri Chretien and then improved upon by Claude Autant-Lara. It wasn't until the 1950s that it really took off.

228 Making movies in colour rather than black and white was attempted throughout the 1920s. Technicolor was invented by Herbert Kalmus from the USA and used a three-colour process that records red, green and blue components of light separately on film. When combined, the three recorded images can reproduce all colours. One of the great examples of an early colour film is *The Wizard of Oz*.

229 Cinerama was a short-lived concept with breathtaking visual effects. Using three cameras, the film could be screened in a panoramic way. However, it was too complicated to shoot many movies under the three-camera system, so the idea was abandoned.

230 In 1832, there was a device that enabled people to see pictures in 3D. It was called the stereoscope and allowed each eye to focus on a separate image. The combined result would give a three-dimensional effect. It was created by Charles Wheatstone and improved upon by David Brewster in 1851.

While it might not scare us now, the sight of a sailing ship and a large white whale in 3D was enough to send anyone running in 1832.

When Francois dropped his piano accordian in the music pit of the movie theatre, the audience assumed the hero had died.

231 Film soundtracks in the early days of silent movies were either played live or recorded on gramophone discs. In 1926, Lee de Forest added a thin strip of soundtrack down the side of the film so words and picture were in sync.

232 Two people on different continents invented stereophonic sound for film in 1933. In the USA it was Harvey Fletcher from the Bell Laboratory and in Britain it was Alan Blumlein.

233 The modern horror 'slasher' movie was a relatively new concept when Alfred Hitchcock introduced the world to *Psycho*, the first movie of its kind.

234 Ray Dolby would not realise how big his name would be one day when he invented the noise reduction system in 1966. This was a simple process that toned down the high frequency hissing on tape recordings.

235 **C**omputer-
generated effects
in movies were
developed in the
early 1980s and
were made
possible due to

computers designed by James Clark. Originally
intending his work for military use, he was surprised
when the movie world embraced the technology to
create fantastic images on-screen.

236 **T**he first full-length CGI (computer generated imagery)
movie was released in 1995. *Toy Story* was made by
Disney and Pixar, and many other films followed.

237 **V**irtual reality is a concept that has been around in
science fiction for years. In 1987, a data glove was
invented by a musician in the USA called Tom
Zimmerman. He wanted to reproduce into a computer
the hand gestures associated with playing an
instrument. The glove is able to copy the movements
of the hand and reconstruct it in a virtual reality
program.

238 **T**he very first
television
commercial aired
in the USA on the
1 July 1941 and
advertised
Bulova clocks
and watches!

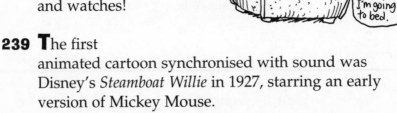

239 **T**he first
animated cartoon synchronised with sound was
Disney's *Steamboat Willie* in 1927, starring an early
version of Mickey Mouse.

240 The first full-length animated feature film was also from Disney. It was *Snow White and the Seven Dwarfs* in 1937.

241 Big Brother was originally a frightening concept thought up by George Orwell for his novel *1984* in which the human race was constantly under surveillance. The TV reality show was an idea inspired by Orwell's vision and came from the mind of John DeMol who took his game show idea to a TV company in the Netherlands. It has since become a worldwide phenomenon.

What do people find so fascinating about watching me fall asleep in a chair. People will watch anything!

Hi, Mum, if you're watching!

I'm changing my socks every day. But then you've probably seen that!

REALITY SHOWS

242 Comic books have their origins in newspaper comic strips. Eventually, comic strips became so popular that they were extended into the comic book format and finally into full graphic novels.

I hate it when people tangle my strings.

243 Puppets as an art form have been around since the ancient Greeks used to perform with shadow puppets. Much later, the stringed variety would come into popular culture and be known as marionettes.

244 The Punch and Judy puppet show is a violent story that has delighted children for centuries. The story and culture has its roots in Italian popular comedy theatre known as 'commedia dell'arte'.

245 Abner Peeler from Iowa in the USA invented the airbrush in 1879. It involved a compressor that sprayed paint and was a crude design. Charles Burdick remodelled and improved the design in 1893.

Abner of Iowa gets creative with his invention THE AIRBRUSH.

246 Roller-coasters were developed by John Miller and his first partner, Norman Bartlett. Built in 1926, the first roller-coaster was known as the 'Flying Turns' ride. Later, Miller would go on to devise further roller-coaster rides with his new partner, Harry Baker.

247 To celebrate the 400th anniversary of Columbus' discovery of America, the World's Fair was held in 1893 in Chicago. A bridge-building engineer named George Ferris was asked to design and build an attraction, and he came up with what is now known as the Ferris wheel.

248 Carousels in some form or another have been around since 500 AD in the Byzantine Empire. Early carousels were very primitive and it wasn't until the late nineteenth century that steam-powered versions appeared in Europe. The early 1900s saw a golden age of the carousel in America where more and more extravagant designs were created.

249 Trampolines are said to have originated from an idea used by the Inuit, who played with stretched walrus skin to toss each other into the air.

Ukluk and his Inuit friends get half way through inventing the trampoline.

However, in 1936 a circus performer named George Nissen built an apparatus in his garage which was the prototype of the modern trampoline.

250 Candy floss/cotton candy/fairy floss has been a part of popular culture since the fifteenth century. In 1897 William Morrison and John Warton from Nashville, Tennessee invented a special machine to easily make it.

251 Bumper cars have been a part of the fun fair for most of the twentieth century. One of the first companies to make them was the Dodgem Corporation, which gave them their nickname of 'Dodgem cars'. The company was founded by a group of previously battling inventors all out to claim the invention as their own.

I don't like the look of this at all! That spinning saw blade looks so real!

It is real!

All I wanted to do was stay at home and vacuum the carpet.

THE SMITH FAMILY TRIES OUT THE SAWMILL RIDE FOR THE FIRST TIME.

252 The amusement park in Texas called 'Six Flags Over Texas' is said to have had the very first Log Flume ride. Built in 1963 by Arrow Development, it was called 'El Aserradero', which is Spanish for 'The Sawmill'.

253 The house of mirrors is often found at carnivals and theme parks. It usually consists of a maze-like path through a room of mirrors. The mirrors can be curved into different shapes, producing distorted reflections. The inspiration for the house of mirrors is thought to be the spectacular hall of mirrors in Palace of Versailles in France, which was completed in 1684.

254 Popcorn, popular with moviegoers and fun park enthusiasts, was originally made by Native Americans and was often flavoured with spices.

255 Toffee apples are a very old tradition. People have been coating fruit in sugar since the mid-nineteenth century, if not earlier. The basic form of a toffee apple is an apple on a stick which has been dipped in molten syrup and left to harden.

Pocahontas... If you'd like a drink with your popcorn let's buy it now...because I don't want to miss the begining of this movie!

CUSTER'S LAST STAND

NOW SHOWING

POPCORN WAS POPULAR AND WAS INVENTED BY NATIVE AMERICANS.

Shopaholic

256 The ancient Lydians were very keen on the idea of marketing. Not only did they invent a monetary system, but they also set up the very first shops back in 600 BC.

257 Although coins had been in existence for centuries, paper money was not used until late in the first millennium. In around 900 AD, paper money began to replace coinage in China, which was becoming a very wealthy country.

258 The bar code was invented by Joseph Woodland and Bernard Silver in 1952. Rather than the recognisable form we know today, it was a number of concentric circles like the rings of a tree.

259 Shopping trolleys or carts were invented in 1936 by an American grocery store owner named Sylvan Goldman.

260 American George Cokely invented the Stop Z-Cart®. This clever shopping cart has a chip inside it, which enables the store owners to keep track of the cart in case it gets stolen.

261 James Ritty invented the first mechanical cash register in 1884. He called it the 'incorruptible cashier'.

262 In 1906, Charles F. Kettering invented a cash register with an electric motor.

263 The founder of the Diners' Club, Frank McNamara, invented credit cards in 1950. The American Express card would follow in 1958.

Frank tries it on with one of the new ATM machines expecting to get money from the machine ...without having a bank account or a card.

264 The ATM (or automated teller machine) was invented by Turkish-born Luther George Simjian in the 1930s, but Don Wetzel developed the more modern and successful machine in 1973.

265 Dee Horton and Lee Hewitt, co-founders of Horton Automatics, invented automatic doors in 1954. They wanted to find a solution to the problem of strong winds blowing doors open.

BOB STOPS TO CHECK THE TIME ON HIS WATCH IN AN OPEN AUTOMATIC DOOR.

266 The ever-fun revolving door was an invention by Theophilus von Kannel in 1888 and is still in use in many shops and hotels today.

267 The Romans were the smart folk who realised that tin cans were perfect for storing and cooking food. They made their cans from copper, rather than tin.

268 Tupperware® was the invention of an American plastics manufacturer named Earl Tupper, who came up with the airtight seal in 1945.

269 The Tupperware® party came next. If it wasn't for the brilliant saleswoman, Brownie Wise, Tupperware® may not have taken off. In the 1950s Brownie came up with the idea of holding parties in people's homes to demonstrate and sell the range of products.

270 The idea of mail ordering came from Richard Sears in 1887 when he began selling watches to American railway workers via post. By 1894, he had teamed up with Alvah Roebuck to produce a large catalogue of items.

271 The supermarket was a slow progression. In 1916, a store in Memphis, Tennessee, allowed customers to pick items off the shelves themselves and bring them to the cash register to pay. In 1930, Michael Cullen opened the first well-stocked grocery store using this system – in an old garage.

272 Internet shopping began in 1995 when Amazon.com sold its very first book in July of that year. Its originator was Jeff Bezos and he started his billion-dollar business in his own garage.

Jeff starts Amazon.com from his garage.

Read All About It!

273 Around 100 BC, the
screw press was
invented. It was able to
forcibly squeeze items
dry or flat or squash
them together. This
would pave the way for
the printing press
centuries later.

274 Shorthand is a simplified form of writing that can be
jotted down quickly when recording someone's
speech. Marcus Tiro came up with the concept in 63 BC
when the Roman politician, Cicero, asked him to
devise a way to capture his every word on paper.

275 The Egyptians used two
forms of writing –
hieroglyphics for formal
occasions and another
script called hieratic,
which was a shortened
version of hieroglyphs
and much faster to
write.

276 Around 50 BC, the Chinese invented paper by dipping
a mesh frame in a mixture of plant fibres and water.
When the mesh was retrieved and left to dry, the
residue on it would form a sheet that was sturdy
enough to write on.

277 The first 'books' were actually scrolls, but over time the length of the scrolls increased, making them more difficult to read. The codex was created around 350 AD. This had pages layered one on top of the other.

278 The woodcut was created in 1400 and was a way of reproducing a picture carved into a wood plate, which was inked and pressed onto paper.

279 In approximately 1455, the metal plate was introduced for the same purpose as the woodcut. These reproductions featured much finer detail.

280 Johann Gutenberg was a jeweller by profession, but his hobby made his name in history as the man who invented the printing press. This enabled pages to be reproduced over and over rather than the old way of people copying material out by hand.

281 The first index to appear in a book was in 1614. It was at the back of the book *Anatomy of the Arts and Sciences*, which was written by Antonio Zara.

282 Henry Cockeram wrote the first dictionary in 1623. It contained only words that he thought people might want to know the meaning of, not everyday words.

I'm making what I call ...the first DICTIONARY. I'll fill it full of words people might want to know the meaning of in 1623. I'll start with, let's say... BUBONIC PLAGUE...and THE BLACK DEATH...

283 In 1702, John Kersey wrote a larger dictionary with meanings of more words. It was the basis for the modern dictionary.

By 1702 John Kersey fights writer's cramp to fit in as many words as possible into his even larger dictionary.

This is just a bad idea!

284 In 1727, a man from Scotland named William Ged made the first 'stereotype'. This was the name given to a metal plate used for printing the pages of a book, so that future prints could be made without setting up that type over and over again.

285 In 1790, tired of the laborious process of hand printing, William Nicholson came up with the idea of the cylinder press, in which an inked roller printed on paper. However, his idea was never actually built.

286 In 1811, this idea was reversed and the paper was wrapped around a cylinder and the type rolled beneath. This system was designed by Germans Friedrich Koenig and Andreas Bauer.

287 The first fully-functioning rotating printing press was developed in 1845 by an American named Richard Hoe.

288 In 1798, Aloys Senefelder invented lithography, the process of transferring images or writing from a plate onto paper via ink and grease.

289 The monotype typesetter was invented in 1885 by Tolbert Lanston and involved a keyboard and a machine that punched the type into soft metal.

290 The linotype machine was invented by Ottmar Mergenthaler in 1886. Rather than setting a letter at a time, it could do a whole row of letters.

291 As the world progressed, new ways of printing came into use. In 1894, phototypesetting was invented by Eugene Porzolt. Letters were projected on a photo-sensitive plate that was then turned into a printing plate. This method wasn't used commercially until the 1950s.

292 The origins of the paperclip (also known as the gem clip) are a bit of a mystery. However, in 1899 William Middlebrook from the USA designed a machine that made the gem clip.

293 The Xerox® machine (or photocopier) was originally invented in 1938 by Chester Carlson of the USA. The process was called xerography and he worked on the idea in his kitchen at home.

Ummm. If only this stove was a copier... I could copy my recipe for Rice Pudding and post it off to Mother.

CHESTER DREAMS OF THE PHOTOCOPIER IN HIS KITCHEN.

294 Desktop publishing owes a lot to PostScript, which is language for writing commands which tell a printer how to lay out images and text on a page. It was invented in 1984 by John Warnock and Charles Geschke, who co-founded the company Adobe.

Sisters Are Doing It for Themselves!

295 Mary Anderson invented the windshield wiper in 1903, when she noticed that drivers had difficulty seeing through the windscreen when it was raining. Her design for a movable arm with a rubber blade was operated from inside the car by a handle.

296 Marion Donovan was tired of having to wash bedsheets after ordinary baby's diapers/nappies leaked, so she improved on these by making new ones with the aid of her shower curtains. The new nappies were waterproof yet washable. Marion's patent was approved in 1951.

297 In 1999 Randice-Lisa Altschul came up with the idea of a disposable mobile phone made of paper that would make outgoing calls up to a certain dollar limit. After that, it would be thrown away or returned for a rebate.

298 Lillian Moller Gilbreth was the inventor of many household items but she is probably best remembered for designing the electric food mixer. The foot pedal bin and shelves on the inside of refrigerator doors were two more of Lillian's brilliant ideas that are commonplace today.

299 Bette Nesmith Graham (who was the mother of Mike Nesmith of The Monkees) invented what she called 'Mistake Out', a white fluid that covered up written mistakes. It is now known as Liquid Paper®.

300 Josephine Cochran invented the dishwasher as she was sick and tired of the fact that no one else had done so! Although she presented her idea back in 1893, it wasn't until about sixty years later that electric dishwashers became domestic items rather than being simply for the catering industry.

301 When Martha Coston's naval scientist husband died, he left an unfinished concept in rough drawings that she would later develop into the flare signal, which has gone on to save thousands of lives. Although Martha originally gave much credit to her husband's initial idea, in 1871 her vast improvements entitled her to a patent all her own.

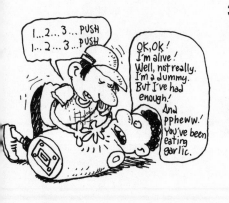

302 Canadian Dianne Croteau and her two colleagues, Richard Brault and Jonathan Vinden, created the dummy on which the CPR treatment is practised. This dummy, known as Actar 911, enables CPR to be demonstrated in the most realistic way without using a human being.

303 Ruth Handler is the creator of the Barbie® doll. She named the doll after her daughter Barbara; in 1965, six years after Barbie's introduction, Ken also came on to the market. He was named after Ruth's son. It has often been stated that every second of every day, somewhere in the world, at least two Barbies are sold.

BARBIE'S MUM PLANS TO DESIGN A DOLL.

Oh Mom! Why do you want to name a doll after me? Everyone will think I'm plastic with synthetic blonde hair!

Ken! Would you like to be a doll then?

304 Finding the ribbed corsets of her day far too painful, New Yorker Mary Phelps Jacob, before heading out to a party in 1910, made a makeshift garment out of two silk handkerchiefs and some ribbon. This became the first prototype brassiere!

305 Amanda Jones, who was also an author, first thought of vacuum packing in tinned food. Her concept was adapted and was called the Jones process. This process meant food would stay fresher for longer.

Now just where did that wee laddy go? The last time I saw him, he was lying on that foldaway bed right about here!

306 In 1885, Sarah Goode invented a foldaway bed which would fit inside a cabinet. It was perfect for guests staying over where the home didn't have enough spare bedrooms.

307 **A**nna Keichline was a fairly prolific inventor and in 1929 she patented an extension of Sarah Goode's foldaway bed, but this one folded away into the wall. Anna was also famous for inventing the K-brick in 1927, which was similar to the concrete bricks we use today in house building.

So Anna... Where's your bedroom in this lovely house of yours?

Oh I don't have a bedroom. I sleep in the wall. In fact, since I invented this fold-up bed the whole family sleeps in the walls.

308 **S**tephanie Kwolek invented Kevlar®, a product which is five times stronger than steel and is used to make bullet-proof jackets.

Vernon, testing the new Kevlar bulletproof vest, has two milliseconds to change his mind about being a test dummy.

309 **A**s far back as 1843, Ada Lovelace thought up concepts which would one day become the modern day computer. She also collaborated with Charles Babbage, who, some would say, invented the first calculating machine.

310 **I**f it hadn't been for the West African women that Ann Moore had seen during her time in the Peace Corps, she would never have had the idea for the baby carrier, which acts as a harness to carry the child on the parent's back. It is known as the Snugli®.

311 **K**rysta Morlan grew up with cerebral palsy. Like other sufferers, she was irritated by wearing casts on her limbs, so in 1977, while in ninth grade, she invented the Cast Cooler, which cooled the space between the cast and skin. While still in high school, she also invented the water bike!

312 **I**n 1898, Lyda Newman of New York came up with the simple yet brilliant idea of a ventilated hairbrush that made it easier to clean and was simple to make.

313 **P**antyhose or tights were the invention of Julie Newmar. She stretched the idea of nylon garments and made snug fitting leg coverings from the material. Julie was perhaps best known for her role as Catwoman in TV's *Batman*.

314 **N**ew Jersey resident Alice Parker took the idea of gas heating and applied it in a new form to a furnace that would provide central heating in homes through air ducts around the building.

315 Scotchguard®, the subtance which is applied to fabric to make it easier to clean (particularly furniture and carpets), was invented by Patsy Sherman from Minnesota in the USA in the early 1950s.

316 While on holiday in Hawaii, Carol Wior invented a swimsuit that would make women look slimmer when they wore it, because of a special lining. Patented in 1990, it is called the Slimsuit.

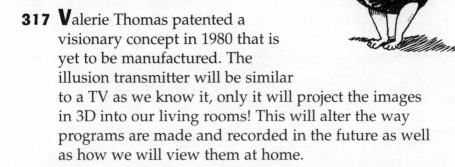

How do I look in this new Slimsuit? Slimmer? Now don't lie!

317 Valerie Thomas patented a visionary concept in 1980 that is yet to be manufactured. The illusion transmitter will be similar to a TV as we know it, only it will project the images in 3D into our living rooms! This will alter the way programs are made and recorded in the future as well as how we will view them at home.

318 Barbara Askins has been credited with improving the X-ray process through the use of radioactive materials. This concept has been invaluable since its introduction back in 1978, as it makes the images much clearer.

319 Krisztina Holly is one of the people behind the first full-colour computer generated hologram (a projection of a 3D image). She did this while she was still at university!

Yes, it's definitely a watch. That would explain the ticking sound. It's right here on the X-ray.

And a nice watch too! Gold I'd say. I had one like that once. But I lost it.

TICK TICK

320 **G**race Hopper was one of the geniuses behind computer language and she also developed COBOL (common business-oriented language) in the 1970s, which is the most common computer language used in business today.

321 **A** system that was patented in 1971 but is still in use today is the computerised telephone switching system. American Erna Schneider Hoover came up with this development in telephone technology.

322 **T**heora Stephens patented the electric pressing-curling iron in 1980 and they were an instant success.

In the 80s... everyone had curling tongs.

323 **T**he ironing board was invented by Sarah Boone, an American, in 1887.

324 **J**oyce Hall was the woman behind Hallmark cards, which began production in 1910 as a mail-order business. Hallmark is now the largest greeting card company in the world.

Getting from A to B

325 Around 4500 years ago, in the colder parts of the northern hemisphere, people invented a simplified version of what we know as skis or snow shoes, in order to easily make their way through the deep snow.

326 The horseshoe was a late invention considering the centuries of riding horses that had gone before. Around 150 BC, leather coverings were strapped to horses' hooves to protect them and help horses walk further more comfortably. Metal shoes with nails were not invented for another 600 years.

327 The magnetic rock magnetite, also known as lodestone, had been used for hundreds of years to navigate but the first recorded use of a magnetised needle that always pointed north comes from 11th century China. By the 13th century the compass was being used by European and Arab sailors.

328 The penny farthing bicycle was invented in 1871 by a British engineer called James Starley and is easily recognised by the small rear wheel and the large front wheel.

329 In 1884, John Stemp-Starley, James' nephew, developed the idea further and designed the now common safety bicycle with its 90-centimetre (36-inch) wheels and chain.

330 Skateboards were invented by surfers, who attached roller skates to plywood boards back in the 1950s. Over the years, the boards were refined. The wheels became smaller, and the axles became stronger.

331 The elevator or lift has been around in some form for centuries. It works by using a pulley system to raise items up and lower them again. It wasn't until 1880 that a German inventor called Werner von Siemens invented the first modern lift.

332 Perhaps one of the most graceful modes of transport is the hot air balloon. The French Montgolfier brothers designed and built their balloon in 1783, and paved the way towards later airships and blimps.

Where is Hans?
I saw him untying the Zeppelin in Berlin.
Oh... never mind! I have found Hans.

333 The Zeppelin company made its first airship in 1900 after spending ten years designing it. Originally airships were filled with hydrogen but this was found to be too dangerous, as hydrogen becomes flammable when combined with air. Helium proved to be a suitable replacement.

334 Who would have thought that the common escalator often found in shopping centres was originally an amusement ride? The very first idea came from Charles Wheeler in 1892 but it wasn't until 1897 that Jesse W. Reno created one for the Coney Island amusement park in New York.

335 In 1919, George Hansburg created a device called the pogo stick, which was a toy for bouncing up and down on. It had a metal frame with a spring inside it, a bar for the feet to stand on and a handle at the top. More recently, the pogo stick has been developed into the Flybar®.

He just bounces around all day long.
So why doesn't he stop?
I don't think he can!

336 Patented in the 1968 by Italian Aquilino Cosani and originally called 'Pon-Pon' was the popular toy now known to many as the spacehopper.

In 1863, James Plimpton stuck one wheel on his shoe... nothing happened. Two wheels... nothing. Three wheels... nothing. Four wheels... he had ROLLER SKATES.

Glad I didn't try that 5th wheel!

337 In 1863 American inventor James Plimpton attached four wheels to each shoe to create the forerunner of the modern-day roller skates.

338 Although horse-drawn wagons ran along wooden railroads in Germany as far back as 1550, it wasn't until 1804 that a man called Richard Trevithick built the first steam locomotive.

Giddee up, Ginger! Technology is catching up with us, old girl.

339 Trevithick's locomotive was similar to the tramway system but it was fellow-Englishman George Stevenson who, with his son Robert, built the first steam-powered railway engine 1825–29.

340 It should be noted that in the early decades of the eighteenth century, two men from England named John Calley and Thomas Newcomen had designed their own form of steam engine. However, it wasn't as efficient as later designs.

341 Two men in different times and places invented the electric motor. English engineer, William Sturgeon, invented the commutator in 1832. An American, Thomas Davenport, also invented one in 1834. This device alternates the current to keep a motor running.

342 The automobile or motor car has a debatable history. There were simultaneous projects around the world working on the concept, and there was a big court case at the beginning of the twentieth century between George Selden, who had patented a multi-cylinder vehicle but never actually completed a finished model, and Henry Ford, who did build his model. Selden lost his patent when the judge ordered a model of his design to be built and it failed to operate!

343 The front-wheel drive seems so obvious to our minds today, but it wasn't invented until 1934, by the two French car designers André-Gustave Citroën and André Lefebvre.

344 Humankind dreamed of being able to fly for thousands of years. In 1903, Wilbur and Orville Wright, two brothers from, Ohio in the USA, made the first successful manned flight. It only lasted twelve seconds but the following year, after alterations and improvements were made, they succeeded in a five-minute flight.

345 The Lockheed Corporation designed pressurised aeroplane cabins in 1937, in order to make flights more comfortable for passengers.

FAUST VRANCIC CHOOSES VENICE TO TEST HIS PARACHUTE IN 1617 AS HE DIDN'T HAVE A LOT OF CONFIDENCE IN HIS INVENTION AND CRASH LANDING INTO WATER FROM A THREE-STOREY BUILDING SEEMED MORE APPEALING THAN LANDING ON SOLID GROUND.

346 **P**arachutes were first drawn by none other than Leonardo Da Vinci. A man from Croatia named Faust Vrancic made a kind of parachute based on the design and tested it out in 1617, in Venice.

347 **I**n 1783, Louis Lenormand from France improved on the parachute design and tested it by jumping off the roof of the Montpelier observatory safely.

348 **T**he first military submarine was designed by an American called David Bushnell in 1776. It was called 'The Turtle'. The submarine was just big enough to hold one man and it submerged by taking water into the hull. It could return to the surface by pumping out the water with a hand pump.

349 **B**oats have been made in many different ways: a hollowed out tree, wood panels bound together with animal skins or, as the ancient Egyptians did over 8000 years ago, fashioned from reeds tied tightly together.

350 **T**he rudder has existed for thousands of years and was used on boats in China. Oars were first used to steer boats, but around 1200 BC one oar was applied to the back of boats as a steering device which became the rudder.

351 The underwater propeller for a ship was invented in 1839 when it was realised that the larger paddlewheels of steam ships were not practical in rougher seas. The idea of the propeller came from two engineers, Swiss John Ericsson and British (Sir) Francis Smith.

Look what I invented. I call it the propeller!

You call that a propeller? This is a propeller! I invented this little baby.

357 The turbine ship was a steam-powered vessel and went a lot faster than ships using pistons. The first one called, 'Turbinia', was launched in 1897.

353 The catamaran was actually the invention of a fishing community in India. The two-hulled boat is held together by a simple frame. The name comes from the Indian word 'kattumaram' which simply means 'logs bound together'.

354 Canals are man-made rivers connecting larger water sources. They have been used to transport boats (barges and riverboats) for many years. The earliest canals date back 6000 years to ancient Mesopotamia.

355 Unicycles are a form of one-wheeled cycle. There is a theory that they were invented shortly after the penny farthing, almost by accident. When a penny farthing hit a bump in the road, it would throw the bike up onto one wheel and the cyclist would precariously balance on it.

You should work in a circus!

Lost your other wheel, mate?

The gentleman I bought this from said this was the last wheel he had left in the store that I could ride away on.

356 The aerial lift is a system whereby passengers are carried high above the ground in a compartment suspended on a thick steel cable running between a number of towers.

357 Scooters come in all shapes and sizes, from those similar to a skateboard with a front handle bar, to the motorised versions related to the motorbike. One of the most successful designs came from Ralph Bonham in 1957, who made the Tote-Gote primarily for himself as he was tired of walking everywhere.

358 An earlier design of scooter came from Italy, in 1946, from a designer called Corradino d'Ascanio. This was the first Vespa®, which is the Italian word for wasp.

359 The first motorbike was the Gottlieb Daimler. It was invented in 1885 but was greatly inspired by the various gasoline-fuelled automobiles and

internal combustion engines designed by Karl Benz, Nicolaus Otto and Henry Ford.

360 The first diesel engine was designed in 1897 by none other than Rudolf Diesel. This engine was more powerful than a regular engine but actually used less fuel.

361 Igniting the fuel in an engine was always a problem until 1902 when G. Honold invented the spark plug, which could control ignition.

362 Leaded petrol was used in car engines after 1921 (before the awareness of pollution). The idea came from Thomas Midgley Jr, who found that adding a lead compound to petrol would make cars run smoother.

363 The rotary internal combustion engine does not have pistons like the other engines, but it has proved more complicated to operate. The engine was invented by Felix Wankel in 1957, but the concept did not take off and the piston engine is still in use today.

364 The Jet Ski® (a registered trademarked name) was designed by Clayton Jacobsen II of Arizona in 1973, who was initially a motocross enthusiast. This is why there are similarities between the Jet Ski and a motorbike!

365 In 1956, Christopher Cockerell invented the first hovercraft, a vehicle that could travel over land and water on a fan-powered cushion of air. However, the idea was not new. In 1716, a Swedish designer named Emanuel Swedenborg came up with the concept but a vehicle was never built.

366 The street car/tram/cable car was invented by Andrew Hallidie who, in 1873, designed a system to pull vehicles up the steep hills in San Francisco in the USA by running wire ropes along channels in the roads. These became the cable cars which are still in use today. There are variations of this design across the world, some using overhead electric cables.

367 The electric trolley bus employed the same electrical motor as used by Werner von Siemens in the electric train. The American Leo Daft designed the system in 1882 and it would remain in use around the world for decades.

368 The induction motor was invented by Nikola Tesla in 1883 and is used in many machines today.

369 The folding bicycle is a bike that can be folded up and stored away or carried. Hans Scholz from the United States designed a compact folding bike in 1989 but there was a patent for a similar idea issued back in 1878 to the man who came up with the spoked bicycle wheel.

Betsy the old girl runs away from a fire faster than running to it! She just hates the smell of smoke.

370 The very first fire engine was horse-drawn and its water was pumped out through a tube using steam power. It was invented by John Braithwaite in 1829 and went through many improvements over the years.

371 Although the Chinese had a flying propeller toy over 2000 years ago and Leonardo Da Vinci drew sketches of a concept in 1490, Paul Cornu invented the modern helicopter in 1907. Unfortunately, his designs were not altogether successful.

Paul, my good friend. Thank you for taking me on your first flight. But I'm finding it a little hard to see the scenery.

Of course! How silly of me! We need a rear tail rotor to stop us from spinning!

THE FIRST HELICOPTER HAD JUST A FEW PROBLEMS

372 An improved helicopter was designed by German scientist Heinrich Focke in 1936 and used two rotors.

373 The single rotor helicopter was designed by Igor Sikorsky from Russia and was an improvement on the two-rotor machine, as it was able to spin around. Sikorsky went on to design the VS-300, which became the major model by 1940.

374 The speedboat is a mixture of different ideas. The boat had been around for a long time. James Watt thought of adding a propeller to the rear in the eighteenth century. However, it was Frederick William Lanchester who, after the invention of the petrol engine in the twentieth century, made the leap and combined all the factors together.

375 The first buses were horse drawn but in Britain in 1831, Goldsworthy Gurney designed steam-powered vehicles influenced by George Stevenson's horse-drawn versions.

376 To combat the problem of over-crowding on buses without having a double-decker, the bendy bus or articulated bus was invented. This is a much longer bus with a flexible middle that doubles the size and is capable of being manoeuvred around corners.

377 John Hetrick patented a design for airbags as far back as 1952. Allen Breed invented a similar design in 1967. Initially just for the driver, they are now fitted into the passenger side of cars. In the event of a collision, the bags will immediately inflate and protect the driver or passenger from hitting their head or chest on anything hard.

378 Inventing a vehicle that moves is impressive enough, but just as important is something to make it stop. Frederick Lanchester invented the disc brake in 1902, and air brakes, used on trains, were the brainchild of George Westinghouse in 1872.

379 The famous 'black box' is really a flight data recorder and isn't, in fact, black at all. An Australian named Dr David Warren invented it and it is an invaluable device that, in the event of a plane crash, can help investigators to determine what went wrong.

380 A Royal National Lifeboat Association inspector in the UK named Captain Ward took the basic idea of a cork flotation blocks as used by Norwegian

seamen and made vests in 1854 for the lifeboat crews. These were for weather protection as well as an aid to buoyancy in the sea.

381 In 1868, London became the first city to install traffic signals similar to ones used for railways. In the USA in 1912, a policeman from Salt Lake City made the first electric signal system that used red and green colours. The third colour, amber, was added later and the first three-colour signal appeared in 1920.

382 In 1923, the 'stop' and 'go' signs in the USA came into use. This system was designed by Garrett Morgan.

383 Pelican crossings (crossings with a set of traffic lights and a walk signal) get their name from the first few letters in the words Pedestrian Light Controlled.

384 Zebra crossings were so nicknamed because of the black and white stripes on the walkway across the road. These pedestrian crossings were introduced to the UK in 1949.

385 The very first subway/metro/underground was the Cobble Hill Tunnel in Brooklyn, New York, in 1850. London's first underground railway opened in 1863.

Hello there, me old matey. Good to smell that French air!

Guten Morgen, Herr Braun! Ich verstehe Sie nicht.

THE CHANNEL TUNNEL FROM ENGLAND TO FRANCE GOES TERRIBLY OFF COURSE ... SOMEWHERE TOWARDS GERMANY.

386 On 1 September 1990, England and France met beneath the English Channel in the brand new Channel Tunnel (or 'Chunnel'). A project that took years to complete, the tunnel is 50 kilometres (31 miles) long with an average depth of 45 metres (41 yards).

387 Once upon a time, the jetpack (a pack worn on the back that uses gas to allow the user to fly) was merely a fantasy. However, many scientists and designers have strived to make the dream come true. Many prototypes have made it to displays including one at the Olympic Games in Atlanta, in the USA.

Woah, Al! I meant to say just go easy on the throttle!

AL TRIES OUT BOB'S JET PACK FOR THE FIRST TIME.

388 SCUBA is an acronym for self-contained underwater breathing apparatus and was coined by the US Navy in 1939. Throughout history, many inventors have attempted to create apperatus for underwater breathing. Some, including Sieur Freminet in France and Henry Fleuss from England, died in the process!

389 The original diving bell, an encased unit that is submerged into water for exploration purposes, was created in 1535 by Guglielmo de Lorena. Interestingly, it was described by Aristotle in the 4th century BC! In 1930, two Americans, William Beebe and Otis Barton, took the idea further and invented the bathysphere, which went on to break depth records.

390 In 1819, Augustus Siebe invented a diving suit that had a helmet attached to a body suit. Someone on the surface of the water pumped air into it via a long tube.

391 The snorkel, although used by swimmers today, was originally a part of a submarine back in 1936. It was invented by Jan Wichers as a way of exhausting fumes and also allowing fresh air in.

392 The aqua-lung was invented in 1943 by Jacques Cousteau and Emile Gagnan, and was the forerunner to the scuba gear.

393 Underwater gear has to be waterproof, obviously. If it wasn't for the research of Frederic Kipping and Eugene Rochow, the waterproof oily compound known as silicone would not have been discovered in 1943.

394 The modern version of wheelchairs were invented in 1932 by engineer Harry Jennings because he had a friend named Herbert Everest who was an invalid. Four hundred years ago, an invalid chair was designed for King Phillip II of Spain.

395 Ambulances were used in their earliest horse-drawn form during conflicts such as the American Civil War (1861–1865) and the French Napoleonic wars (1799–1815).

396 Sir Frank Whittle of Britain and Hans von Ohain of Germany invented the turbo jet engine in the 1930s. However, they never worked together and didn't know of the other's designs.

397 The turboprop engine uses jet propulsion and a propeller, resulting in a more efficient way of flying than the old piston engines. Vickers Armstrong Aircraft developed it in 1953.

398 The Concorde began as a collaborative design between the British, French, Americans and Soviets in an attempt to develop supersonic air transport back in the 1950s. Because the project was so expensive, it took a couple of decades to get it up in the air. The first Concorde commercial flight was not until 1976 and the last one was in 2003, when the planes were retired.

399 The wheel is renowned for being one of our earliest inventions. It enabled people to move large objects, create pulley systems and, eventually, travel great distances with ease.

400 One of the first wheeled vehicles was the chariot around 3500 BC. It was to continue to be invaluable means of transport for many centuries.

401 Rickshaws have been in use in Japan since 1868. The passenger sits in a sheltered seat above two large wheels and a man pulls from the front as he runs. The original rickshaw inventor is unknown, but it may have been an American named Jonathan Scobie, whose wife was an invalid. He needed some form of transport for her while they were in Japan.

402 In 1933, a Yorkshire man named Percy Shaw designed a reflective device called the 'cat's eye', placed on roads to guide drivers in bad weather or at night. These devices got their name from the fact that real cats' eyes reflect in the same way.

403 Before the invention of the compass, a Chinese army under emperor Huang-ti in the third millennium BC used a carriage bearing a small statue that always pointed south. A system of gears linked to the wheels kept the statue facing south no matter which way the carriage moved.

404 An Italian named Petrus Vesconte made the first dated navigational chart in 1311. It covered the area of the Mediterranean Sea. It wasn't thoroughly accurate, as it wasn't created using actual measurements.

405 Horse riders have been using saddles to make riding easier for a long time, even if they were little

more than a blanket folded and placed on the horse's back. Eventually, leather saddles were invented. They were more durable and far more comfortable for both horses and riders.

406 Wheelbarrows were, oddly, a rather late invention. They didn't appear until sometime during the first century. They were used initially by European workmen and miners.

407 Truss bridges (where the supports form a triangular shape) are far more capable of withstanding weight than a simple flat bridge. The Romans built truss bridges to support the weight of many men in order to cross rivers at the turn of the second century.

SHORTLY BEFORE THE COMPLETE COLLAPSE OF A ROMAN TRUSS BRIDGE INTO A FLOODED RIVER SOMEWHERE IN GAUL IN THE SECOND CENTURY.

408 The first iron bridge was designed by Thomas Pritchard and was built by Abraham Darby in 1779. It crossed the River Severn in Shropshire, England, and it still stands today.

409 The earliest caterpillar tracks (a series of metal units formed into a belt, then fitted over wheels) were designed by Richard Edgeworth in 1770. They were used in the Crimean War in the 1850s. An adapted design was successfully made by Alvin Lombard in 1901.

410 Sir Isaac Newton discovered the principle of the sextant in the early 1700s, a tool to aid navigation. However, two men rediscovered the concept around 1730 and developed it – an American named Thomas Godfrey and an Englishman named John Hadley.

411 Canal locks are ingenious devices for raising and lowering canal boats from one water level to the next. They have been around since the late fourteenth century.

412 The hang-glider was originally an idea from NASA. It was suggested as a way for astronauts to safely return to the Earth's surface. Technician Francis Rogallo set about creating the contraption in 1948. Further developments continued in Australia, where the concept was perfected. Hang-gliding is now a popular sport.

413 At the beginning of the 1960s, a parachutist called Pierre Lemoigne invented the paraglider by cutting strips in his parachute in order to control airflow through the canopy and enable steering. In 1962, Englishman Walter Newark perfected this design. Parasailing became a popular sport by the 1970s.

After two years on the rocky island of Pharos, Amenhotep falls asleep dreaming of lying in the hot sand under palm trees on the bank of the Nile ... and lets the lighthouse fire go out.

CRUNCH

414 The lighthouse has been invaluable to travellers of the high seas. The first specifically built lighthouse was in Egypt, on the island of Pharos, around 280 BC. Its light was a blazing fire at the top of a set of stairs.

415 In 1759, engineer John Smeaton, weary of the damage caused to previous lighthouses in bad weather, cemented stones together and built the Eddystone lighthouse in England.

416 The very first boat with an iron hull was built in 1787. It was designed by John Wilkinson. The boat was a barge and travelled its first journey down the River Severn in England.

417 Robert Fulton from the USA invented the first successful steam ship in 1807. Many others attempted to do so but they managed only a few voyages before complications arose – like falling to pieces from the tremendous vibrations of their engines.

Is the ship still taking water, Jones? Report back to me if there is any change.

Yes, Captain! Those rivets appear to be vibrating loose and we are taking on water sir.

418 In 1827, Scottish engineer John McAdam invented a more durable road surface by using soil with stones scattered on top. These roads were in common use until cars became popular. Then the stones had to be made firmer by using tar.

419 Tyres on cars are made of durable rubber. The process used to make the rubber is called vulcanisation and it was developed by Charles Goodyear in 1839. His name is now often associated with tyres.

420 In 1929, Germans Walter Bock and Eduard Tshunkur invented a synthetic rubber for tyres.

421 The idea of organising trips and tours through a travel agent started back in 1841 when Thomas Cook invented the package holiday. The very first one was a trip from Leicester to Loughborough, in England. The company still bears his name.

422 The very first tunnel to go under a waterway travels under the River Thames in London and is still used today. It was designed and built by Marc Brunel and his son Isambard. Started in 1825, it took eighteen years to build.

423 In 1865, George Pullman and Ben Field worked together to design a train compartment with bunk beds so that people could sleep on long journeys.

WHILE DRIVING HAPPILY UNDER THE THAMES RIVER....

424 In 1879, Werner von Siemens from Germany built the first prototype electric train, although it only went around in a circular track. It

quickly became a popular type of transport and eventually replaced the steam engine.

425 It doesn't seem likely that a boat made out of paper would be of much use, does it? In 1867 a father and son team, Elisha and George Waters, began making boats from paper, which was then varnished. These boats were light and fast, and won many races. Eventually they were replaced by fibreglass boats.

Father and son boat designing and racing team Elisha and George Waters test one of their paper boats.

426 The monorail in Wuppertal, Germany, is one of the earliest and it still stands today. It was created by Eugen Langen in 1901.

427 The first glass windows in cars were very dangerous as they could shatter and become lethal to someone in the car during an accident. Laminated safety glass was designed by an artist from France named Edouard Benedictus. It was made up of two sheets of glass with plastic cemented between them.

428 The British army were the first to produce a workable tank in 1915. Army engineers were inspired by armour-plated cars, first seen in 1914.

429 All vehicles must be parked sometime and the parking meter was an obvious invention. It first made its appearance in 1935 in the USA and was invented by a man named Carlton Magee.

430 When flying at great speeds there is the problem of g-force (the effect of acceleration), which can cause passengers to blackout. The anti-g suit was invented by Wilbur Franks in 1940 in Canada. Made of two layers of rubber with a thin filling of water in between, the suit maintained the equilibrium of the body during flights.

431 Another important invention where aircraft is concerned is that of carbon fibre, as it is very light. Leslie Phillips invented carbon fibre in 1963. It forms a plastic when heated that is as strong as steel but also practical and light.

432 If you are planning to drive from A to B, it is strongly advised that you don't attempt it under the influence of alcohol. The breathalyser was invented in 1954 by Robert Borkenstein. It had a chemical in it that changed colour if alcohol is present in the bloodstream.

433 The seat belt was designed as an anchor to prevent people from being injured when a vehicle comes to a sudden stop. Nils Bohlin from Sweden designed the strap we know so well today and it was first used in a Volvo in 1959.

434 The jump jet is able to take off vertically due to jet thrusters that point downwards. The British Hawker Siddeley Aviation Company was the first to make the Harrier jump jet in 1960.

435 Radar has made it difficult for planes to travel without being detected. The stealth aircraft was a product of hard work by the Lockheed Martin Corporation in 1983. The idea was to design a craft that would not reflect the radar back to the source but rather absorb it or deflect it in another direction.

You could call me a Top Gun fighter pilot, I suppose. And this is my little baby here. Fully remote control and only 12cm across from wingtip to wingtip! And I don't even need to move out of my armchair to fly it.

436 The Lockheed Martin Corporation also created the MicroSTAR air reconnaissance plane in 1998. It was only 15 centimetres (6 inches) across and weighed 85 grams (3 ounces), but it could carry a tiny camera and transmitter.

437 The sailboard for windsurfing was an idea patented in 1968 by a couple of surfers named Jim Drake and Hoyle Schweitzer.

Jim invents the SAILBOARD... and goes wherever the wind takes him ... Somewhere out into the Pacific Ocean.

438 The first human powered aircraft was the Gossamer Albatross. It was made of light plastics and had a pedal-powered cockpit. It took flight in 1977 and was flown across the English Channel by Bryan Allen.

BRYAN PEDALS HIS WAY ACROSS THE ENGLISH CHANNEL

439 The GPS, or Global Positioning System, was launched in 1978. It uses satellites to figure out where you are precisely.

440 The ice bike was invented in 2003 by Dan Hanebrink and Doug Stoup as an alternative to cross-country skiing. It has no plastic parts, as they would only freeze and crack. It also has fatter wheels than a normal bike.

441 Dean Kamen invented the Segway Human Transporter in 2001. It is powered by electricity and it is self-supporting, as it houses five gyroscopes. It only travels at 19 kilometres (12 miles) per hour and has no brakes, but it is an interesting adaptation of the scooter.

442 The Maglev train works using electromagnetic energy supported by a magnetic field. It hovers above the track. Because it is not actually touching the rails, there is less friction and the train can go at higher speeds. These trains are used in Japan and China. British engineer Eric Laithwaite developed the technology behind this in 1948.

Fun, Games and Sport

443 **D**ice were an early invention from around 4000 years ago. They did not always have dots – some had runes or other symbols. Dice were often used as a way of telling the future.

444 **C**luedo® (or 'Clue' as it is known in America) was invented by Anthony Ernest Pratt from Birmingham, England in 1943 – although it wasn't published by Waddington's games until 1949.

445 **M**onopoly® has a confusing history with lawsuits surrounding the claims as to who actually invented it. Some say it was Charles Darrow in 1930 and some say it was Lizzie Magie in 1906. Maybe we will never learn the truth!

446 **T**wo Canadians named Scott Abbott and Chris Haney invented Trivial Pursuit® in 1979, but it was a couple of years before it was released to the general public. During the 1980s it became a worldwide phenomenon.

447 **I**n the 1930s, Alfred Butts devised a game in which players would put together words with letters written on small cardboard squares. Over time, the game was known as 'Lexico', 'It' and 'Criss-cross'. It became Scrabble® in 1948.

448 **B**ingo originated in Italy in 1530, where it was a form of lotto. Early versions of the game in the USA were called 'Beano' because beans were used to cover up the numbered squares.

DONATELLO HAS A BIG WIN AT THE FIRST BINGO HALL IN ITALY IN 1530.

449 **C**hess is around 4000 years old and originated in Persia and India. However, it wasn't until the 1840s that a super chess champion named Howard Staunton designed the pieces we play with today.

450 **S**occer is one of the earliest versions of the game of football known to man and there are many historical references to the game in China, Greece and Italy. Today's game, and its rules, date back to nineteenth-century England when it was popular with boys' schools.

Chen's father Yang-Tse buys him a soccer ball from a sports store on his way home from his job building the Great Wall of China ... and Chen invents the game of Soccer.

451 **B**asketball was invented by an American teacher called James Naismith in 1891. He took a basket and a regular football into the gymnasium, and attempted to pitch the ball into the goal.

452 **T**he French invented the first form of tennis in the twelfth century, although it was then called 'Paulme' meaning 'palm' because the ball was struck with the palm of the hand.

THE SCOTS INVENT GOLF IN THE 15th CENTURY.

453 Golf can be traced back to a game played by the Scots in the fifteenth century. Players would use sticks to hit small stones on sand dunes!

454 Rugby is a sport that takes its history from the game of soccer and has two separate forms, Rugby League and Rugby Union. Legend has it that, in 1823, William Webb Ellis, a young player of the game at Rugby School, in England, picked up the ball and ran with it. Rugby is the forerunner of American football.

455 American football was given its own rules in 1879 by a football coach named Walter Camp. Along with baseball, it is now one of their biggest sports.

456 Ice skates have been discovered dating back as far as 3000 BC! Made from animal bone with leather straps, they were found in a lake in Switzerland.

Oh yes! We gave Cragg a set of Woolly Rhinoceros Thigh Bone Ice Skates for his birthday just as the ice formed on the lake and we haven't been able to keep him off them!

457 The first mechanically refrigerated ice skating rink was built in Chelsea, England, in 1876. John Gamgee was the builder and he named it the Glaciarium.

458 Baseball was around in the early nineteenth century in America but the modern baseball field and the first rules were invented by Alexander Cartwright in 1845, which have evolved into the modern game.

459 Ice hockey was been around in Europe for centuries but the rules in use today were devised by Canadian J. G. A. Creighton, in 1875.

460 A young man named William Morgan from Massachusetts invented the game of volleyball in 1895. He originally named it 'mintonette'.

461 Cricket has a very long history, dating as far back as 1300. It is said to have originated in the south of England and was played by farmers. Now cricket is one of the most popular sports in the world.

EARLY CRICKET

462 Paintball has a surprising history, as it was not invented as a sport. Forestry commissioners designed a gun that emitted paint pellets for marking trees in areas difficult to access. The game evolved after some of the people marking the trees started fooling around and firing at each other!

463 The Olympic Games as a concept has been around for centuries. The first recorded games were in 776 BC in ancient Greece. The modern games began in 1896 and are generally held every four years.

THE FIRST OLYMPIC GAMES IN ANCIENT GREECE.

464 The Commonwealth Games started in 1930, and were then called the British Empire Games. This competition is also held every four years. The competing countries are all part of the British Commonwealth.

465 Othello®, a simple yet brilliant game of skill, was invented by Goro Hasegawa from Japan in 1971. It has been an addictive game ever since.

466 Sudoku was originally invented by an American, suitably named Howard Games, in 1979 for a New York newspaper. It started a massive craze in Japan when introduced there in 1984. The name 'sudoku' roughly translates to 'single numbers'.

467 Snakes and ladders has an unknown inventor but it is said to have been one of the first popular board games. It was invented in 1870.

468 In 1971, a barber named Merle Robbins adapted the game that was to become Uno® from a simple deck of cards. Uno went on to become one of the biggest card games in the world.

469 Although the game of dominos has a heavily Chinese-influenced history, the first appearance of the modern game was in Italy during the eighteenth century.

470 John Spilsbury was a mapmaker in London. In 1767, he took his wood-mounted map and then cut it up into smaller pieces in an attempt to make an educational toy. This was the very first jigsaw puzzle.

471 The very first crossword puzzle, originally called a 'word-cross' puzzle, was featured in the *New York World* newspaper in December 1913. It was devised by Liverpool-born Arthur Wynne, who had immigrated to America.

472 One of the largest selling toys ever is the Rubik's Cube®, which was invented by Erno Rubik. A true brainteaser, the Rubik's Cube was a huge craze during the 1980s, with many of Rubik's spin-offs and other brand wannabes filling the toyshops.

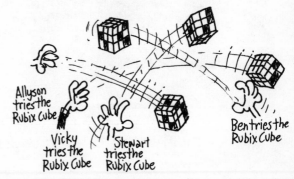

473 Cabbage Patch Kids® were an invention by a young man named Xavier Roberts when he was just a teenager in 1976. The name 'Cabbage Patch Kids' was adopted when the Coleco Company marketed Xavier's dolls in 1983 and they became a world-wide phenomenon.

What's that, Maryanne? That's just a cabbage with some stick-on eyes.

Hmmmm, thought I was going to get away with that one!

AFTER MISSING OUT ON A CABBAGE PATCH KID FOR HER BIRTHDAY... MARYANNE TRIES THE NEXT BEST THING.

474 Invented by Bonnie Zacherle, Charles Muenchinger and Steven D'Aguanno, the patent for My Little Pony® was granted in 1983 and the toy was distributed through Hasbro Toys.

475 Arthur Granjean from France invented the Etch-a-Sketch® in 1959 but it wasn't marketed until the 1960s.

476 Although hoops have been used as a toy for many centuries, the term Hula Hoop® was trademarked in 1958 by the Wham-O company.

477 Whoopee cushions were invented around the 1940s when some workers at the Jem Rubber Co. of Canada were playing about with some scrap sheets of rubber. The rest is history!

Don't be so rude, Albert! And at the dinner table too!

If only those guys who invented the Whoopee cushion back in Canada in the 1940s knew of the embarrassment and humiliation they've caused me tonight!

BBRRRR

LAW ENFORCEMENT TRIALS A NEW STINK BOMB

478 It is not known who exactly invented the practical joke in the form of the stink bomb, but the military have been known to experiment to find the smelliest substance known to man, to be used in law enforcement!

479 The yo-yo is one of the oldest toys in the world, often used in ancient Greece. In the Philippines, the yo-yo was much larger and sharper, and was used as a hunting weapon. It wasn't until the 1920s that the yo-yo toy became popular with the general public.

480 A toy that went down but didn't go up again is the spring-inspired Slinky®. It was invented by Richard and Betty James in 1945 after Richard noticed how a tension spring he was working with continued to move after it had fallen to the ground.

481 Mr Potato Head® was invented in 1952 by George Lerner from New York and was eventually manufactured by Hasbro Toys.

482 Noah and Joseph McVicker were in their twenties when they invented the modelling clay that was to become Play-doh®, although originally they were trying to make wallpaper cleaner. Hasbro marketed it in 1956.

WHILE FUMBLING FOR A LIGHTSWITCH IN THE DARK WHILE WORKING BACK LATE ONE NIGHT AT THE OFFICE, JAMES STUMBLES OVER A DRUM OF SILICONE OIL AND A PACKET OF BORIC ACID. HE FELT SILLY FOR STANDING IN THE PUTTY... BUT PUT THE 'SILLY' AND THE 'PUTTY' TOGETHER AND SOON BECAME A MILLIONAIRE.

483 **A**nother fun, pliable toy is Silly Putty®. An engineer named James Wright stumbled upon this strange plastic when mixing boric acid with silicone oil. It was sold as Silly Putty in 1949 and at the time was the fastest selling toy in history.

484 **L**ego® and Legoland® came from the mind of Godtfred Christiansen, whose father owned a toy-making company. In 1934, the company was renamed 'Lego', which came from the Danish phrase 'Led godt' which means 'Play well'.

485 **D**avid Brewster from Scotland invented the kaleidoscope in 1816. Combining a tube with mirrors and glass plates inside it, as well as coloured fragments, he made a fascinating toy which would create infinite different patterns when turned.

486 **T**he frisbee has had many claiming to be its original inventor but the most likely tale is the one of the Frisbie Pie Company, which delivered

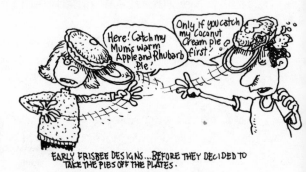

EARLY FRISBEE DESIGNS... BEFORE THEY DECIDED TO TAKE THE PIES OFF THE PLATES.

pies to students at colleges in New England, in the USA. The tin tray left behind after the pie was eaten was often thrown around for fun.

487 **S**ubbuteo is the game otherwise known as table football. It involves moving toy players on rods and knocking the ball into the other player's goal. Peter Adolph invented it in 1947.

488 Frank Hornby originally patented Meccano® as 'Mechanics Made Easy' in 1901. The trademarked name Meccano was registered in 1907.

489 The electronic robotic pet, Furby®, was invented by Richard Levy and was first marketed in 1998. It soon became a much-desired toy for children across the world.

490 The Spirograph® was invented by Denys Fisher in 1965 and is a toy for drawing geometric shapes and patterns.

Daddy! I've learnt to draw on my new Spirograph. It's so easy! This drawing is of a girl chasing butterflies in a garden with a small dog called Freddie. What do you think of it?

Well... Let's just say ...it's interesting.

491 Tamagotchi® is a virtual pet and was designed by a Japanese inventor named Aki Maita in 1996.

492 Another robotic pet was the Aibo®, which was invented by Toshitada Doi from Japan. These toys were first introduced at the Toy Fair in 2001. They can imitate real-life creatures and even show emotions.

eeep eeep eeep eeep eeep

Oh no! My little electronic pet has just died!

But thanks to the wonders of modern technology, I'll just stick in new batteries... and it will be alive again.

493 The toy known as Jacob's Ladder has unknown origins. Its design of wooden blocks that seem to cascade down past each other has amused children for years.

494 Poker has a very complicated history and it is not definite where the origins of the game lie. However, it may be connected to the French game 'Poque' or the English game 'Brag'. Today it is more popular than ever, even being played on a television program as a spectator sport!

495 The Fitness Corporation invented the Abdominizer® (a stomach workout device) in 1982. However, many people managed to injure themselves while using one, so better models had to be made to overcome these problems.

A POINTLESS RACE AT THE GYM.

496 Exercise bikes have changed in style over the years, though nowadays the bikes can be adjusted to varying degrees of speed and pressure.

497 The cross-trainer is designed to exercise different parts of your body at once. There are various designs but all have the same purpose of improving the cardio-vascular system and muscle tone.

After spending a solid four hours on the crosstrainer at the gym to move 10kg of stubborn fat from his waistline... Stewart can't move a muscle.

I can't even move my jaws to tell anyone that I can't move a muscle!

498 Treadmills enable people to run without leaving the room. They can control the speed of the conveyor belt and the incline of a hill through the push of a button.

While using his brand new POWER TREADMILL Harry notices a shoe lace undone... bends over to tie it up and... WHAMMm!

499 Gym balls, also known as Swiss balls or fit balls, are relatively new pieces of gym equipment. When used, the body tries to balance with the ball, exercising the stomach and back muscles to work as they should. Some people substitute their chair at work with a gym ball to aid their posture.

Hey...take a seat on my gym ball and make yourself comfortable and I'll pop off and make us a coffee. White with one sugar, isn't it?

500 Rowing machines simulate the actions you would make if rowing a boat on water. They are a great way of building upper body strength.

501 Swimming pools have been around since ancient Greek and Roman times. In 1837, six indoor pools were built in London and it was the modern Olympic Games in 1896 that inspired more people to use pools.

502 Sunscreen or suntan lotion was made in 1936 by Eugene Schueller and was an oil to prevent the skin being burnt by the harmful rays of the sun. Today, his company is known as L'Oreal.

503 **A**cupuncture is an incredibly old method of healing. It began in China around 4500 years ago and involved piercing the skin with needles (back then, they were made of stone) in order to help the person's 'chi' (life force) flow more easily.

504 **A**romatherapy is a method of alternative medicine and the concept has been around for a possible 9000 years! Many ancient civilisations, including the Egyptians, used aromatic oils and incense in the healing process.

NEFERHOTEP EXPERIMENTS WITH MOULDY HIPPOPOTAMUS DUNG AROMATHERAPY FOR THE PHARAOH'S INGROWN TOENAIL.

505 **I**t is likely that yoga as a meditative form is over 7000 years old. The principles of yoga are mentioned in the Hindu scriptures, the Upanishads, which date back over 3000 years.

506 **K**arate is a form of martial arts invented by the Chinese. The name 'Karate-do' translates to 'the way of the open hand'.

507 **J**udo is not only a martial art, but it is also a philosophy that comes from the Japanese culture. Its founder was Kano Jigoro towards the end of the nineteenth century.

Hard at Work

508 The word 'tractor' is most often associated with the machine/vehicle seen on farms around the world. The name comes from the Latin word 'trahere' which means 'to pull'.

509 The plough is one of the oldest farming tools. The earliest plough was a basic hoe that could be pulled through the soil by people or animals. The modern versions are much more complex and have two separate blades.

510 Bulldozers are large caterpillar-tracked tractors with a strong blade at the front for pushing and demolishing things. They came into use in the 1930s in the USA.

511 The bulldozer was inspired by the Fresno Scraper, which was invented in 1883 by James Porteous. He saw the need to design a machine that would scoop the earth rather than just pushing it away when making waterways for irrigation.

512 A compactor, or rotor-compactor, does exactly as its name suggests. It is a heavy drum that compacts things by crushing them under its weight. The machine is often used when making new roads.

513 Through a system of cables, hydraulics and pulley systems, the crane can support great weights and lift huge items to great heights. Skyscrapers would be very difficult to build without the use of large, modern cranes.

514 Dragline excavators have a crane-like extension but they also carry a bucket that scoops rubble from the ground They are a very useful tool in mining.

Has anybody seen my car? It was here a minute ago!

515 The excavator has a similar purpose to a dragline excavator. However, it has an extended jointed arm that moves in a manner resembling a human arm. Giant excavators are used in the mining industry, making mining safer and quicker.

516 Feller bunchers are, once again, very like tractors, except they have a tree-cutting saw at the front. They are used for harvesting trees in forests.

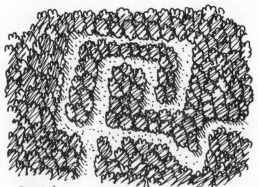

Bored with harvesting trees straight up and down Rich decides to get creative with his Feller buncher tractor.

517 Giant harvesters also used for felling trees and can also transport the fallen logs.

518 **F**orklift trucks are another type of lifting machine that relies heavily on hydraulics. At the front of the vehicle there are two rigid arms that can be placed under heavy objects and then be raised to lift them and move them. Forklift trucks are used in factories world-wide.

519 **F**ront loaders and backhoe loaders are forms of tractor that have a scoop for digging. The latter also has a large hoe-like device at the rear.

520 **G**raders are large machines that level earth to a reasonably flat surface through the action of an enormous blade that drags along the ground.

521 **A** very early form of industrial vehicle was the threshing machine. It was invented by Andrew Meikle in 1788 and was able to hold all the wheat that it threshed.

522 **R**eaping harvests was a tiresome job that required many people. In 1826, Patrick Bell from Scotland invented a reaping machine with a large reel that turned in the ground and

lifted the wheat and corn into the shredder.

523 **E**mil Lerp invented the chainsaw in 1927. It ran on petrol/gasoline and the rotating chain acted like a saw blade. The one drawback was that it was too heavy, so in 1950 a lighter version was created by Andreas Stihl.

CCCRUNCH

With the invention of the new lighter weight chainsaw, it meant Max could go chop things down just about anywhere.

524 **I**n 1984 builders on construction sites found a new way of sending rubbish down from great heights. Before the dust-free chute – which is a collection of linked tubes – builders had to use makeshift chutes out of planks, and debris would go all over the place.

525 **W**elding dates back centuries and involves joining metals through intense heat. An iron pillar in India that was erected around the year 310 shows evidence of welding.

Doctor, Doctor!

526 Wilhelm Conrad Rontgen discovered X-rays in 1895 when he found an image had been cast by his cathode ray generator. He took the first X-ray photograph . . . of his wife's hand!

527 MRI stands for magnetic resonance imaging and is a method of seeing inside the body for medical purposes. Raymond Damadian invented the first MRI scanner in 1970.

528 The first full body image taken with an MRI machine was in 1977. A US scientist called Paul Lauterbur also contributed to the success of the MRI machine.

529 Godfrey Hounsfield and Allan Cormack were individually working on the idea of the CAT-scan during 1972. In 1975, X-ray technology helped Robert Ledley to patent the CAT-scan machine, which can take 3D X-rays.

530 The PET (positron emission tomography) scanner is a machine that can see inside the human body and brain, and show events within. It reads electrons and positrons to produce images. The machine was designed by Michael Phelps and Edward Hoffman in 1974.

531 Trepanation was a prehistoric idea that has been used throughout human history. It has little scientific basis and involves drilling holes into the skull in order to release disease or mental disorder.

532 In 1853, two scientists, Charles Gabriel Prevaz and Alexander Wood, came up with a syringe that could safely pierce the skin of a human. Injections and infusions had been around since 1670; this was the first hypodermic syringe.

533 Aspirin was a discovery by Felix Hoffman in 1899 when he saw that his father use salicylic acid, the ingredient in aspirin, to help his rheumatism.

534 In 1865, Joseph Lister found that cleaning an operating theatre with carbolic acid helped maintain a sterilised area. This was the forerunner of antiseptic.

535 The first hospital for the public was probably built around the end of the fourth century in Rome. It was the idea of a woman who would eventually be made a saint. St Fabiola went on to build many more hospitals.

536 Spectacles have a debatable history. Some say the use of magnifying lenses for improved sight may date back to the Chinese in the tenth century, but the actual eyewear itself may not have come into existence until the end of the thirteenth century.

Barnabas...I've never seen you look so thin. Did they have the plague in your village?

Elias tries out a pair of newly invented spectacles.

537 Bifocal spectacles were invented by Benjamin Franklin. In his later years he had difficulty using his reading glasses for everyday use, so he invented a double lens pair of spectacles through which he could read when looking down and see distances when looking straight ahead.

538 In 1792, Dominique Larrey, a doctor in the Napoleonic wars in France, invented the flying ambulance, which was actually a highly mobile medical team that could quickly see to the wounded.

The new flying ambulance arrives just in the nick of time for Pierre who lay in a trench on the battlefield not knowing whether he was Pierre, Napolean Bonaparte or the Eiffel Tower (Mind you... He wasn't the Eiffel Tower...it hadn't been built yet.)

539 Edward Jenner discovered the smallpox vaccination in 1798. He realised that those who had cowpox didn't catch smallpox, so the first vaccine to the killer disease infected people with the cowpox virus.

540 Toothpaste was around in the nineteenth century and was bought by the jar. A dentist named Washington Sheffield first had the idea to market it in a tube but it was William Colgate's dental cream that would surpass it in 1896.

541 **N**itrous oxide, or 'laughing gas' as it is more commonly known, was discovered by Humphrey Davy in 1799. Although it would later be used in the surgery, Davy also made his parties more entertaining (and dangerous) by making his guests laugh.

542 **T**he stethoscope was invented by Rene Laennec in 1819 simply because he was too embarrassed to place his ear so close to a stranger's chest!

543 **T**wo French chemists named Joseph Caventou and Pierre Pelletier were responsible for discovering quinine, which was useful when treating malaria. They also discovered the anaesthetic alcohol, chloroform.

544 **A**naesthetics were first used by dentists in 1846. Laughing gas was attempted but wasn't completely successful. Ether was a popular choice as it could knock the patient out. A Scottish doctor named James Simpson eventually used chloroform for women in labour in 1847.

545 **L**ouis Pasteur was the man who, in 1865, realised that living organisms within foodstuffs could cause disease. His process of destroying the organisms was called pasteurisation.

546 Louis Pasteur also came up with the vaccination for rabies in 1885. Long before this, there were myths about how to cure people who had been bitten by a rabid dog. One was to chew the hair of the dog that bit you. This didn't work but gave us the saying, 'The hair of the dog'.

547 Thermometers for medical use were introduced in 1866. They were smaller and easier to handle than the usual domestic thermometer.

548 Sterilisation is very important in the operating theatre in order to keep bacteria from getting into the open body. In 1886, Ernst von Bergmann had the idea of steaming all of his instruments in order to kill off germs, thus saving many lives.

549 Continuing the theme of sterilisation, William Halsted from America invented extremely thin, yet strong, rubber gloves to wear when performing surgery. These are still in use today.

550 To prevent infection from tetanus, two scientists named Emil Behring and Kitasato Shibasaburo came up with an immunisation. It was a heated or chemically treated poison from the original virus and acted as a vaccine.

551 Surgical masks were an idea of Jan Mikulicz-Radecki who realised in the late 19th century that germs could come from the surgeon's mouth so he placed a piece of gauze over his mouth when operating.

I can't-a find-a any blood pressure! If I can't-a find-a any blood pressure it means-a you're dead! I pump-a this a little tighter and-a see what-a happens.

552 Doctors use an instrument called a sphygmomanometer to measure blood pressure. An Italian, Scipione Riva-Rocci, invented this device in 1896.

553 Marie Curie was the first female Doctor of Science in Europe. Most of her work was shared with her husband, Pierre, until his death in 1906. Through her work and research into radiotherapy, she also became the first woman to win the Nobel Prize in 1903. She won a second in 1910.

554 In 1901 an Austrian named Karl Landsteiner discovered that there were different types of blood groups and that mixing the wrong sorts during a transfusion could actually kill a patient.

555 Johnson & Johnson employee Earle Dickson in the USA made self-adhesive dressings in 1920 by placing pieces of gauze onto sticky tape. He then rolled them up and sold them as Band-aids®.

In 1920 Earle Dickson finds many uses for his new adhesive dressings.

556 Insulin is used to control diabetes and was discovered by Frederick Banting and Charles Best in 1921.

557 Fred Sanger and Dorothy Hodgkin discovered the structure of insulin in 1969. This important breakthrough helped scientists form a synthetic variety.

558 Penicillin was discovered by Alexander Fleming in 1928 when he found that bacteria didn't survive when placed near some mould. His work was continued by Ernst Chain and Howard Florey. By the 1940s penicillin was in regular use, especially during World War Two.

559 Hans Berger of Germany invented the electroencephalograph (or EEG) in 1920 to record brain activity. This device is a system of electrodes that are placed on the head to read electrical activity.

560 The iron lung was an invention by Phillip Drinker and Louis Agassiz Shaw in 1927. The original design was operated using a couple of vacuum cleaners and a large, iron-sided casket.

CHUGGA CHUGGA PUMP PUMP

This is the best artificial heart we can give you in 1952, Mr Smith. But don't worry about its size. It fits nicely onto a small trailer you can tow behind you wherever you go.

561 The pacemaker is a life-saving device that uses electrical impulses to keep a patient's heart beating. An early design in 1952 by Paul Zoll was too heavy to move around, so in 1957 Earl Bakken designed a smaller battery-powered one.

562 In 1998, Brandon Whale, aged ten, invented a device called the Pace Mate. This was an elasticised version of the sensor-bracelet worn by his mother after she had a pacemaker fitted. By adding electrolyte sponges that helped to conduct the electricity, Brandon's mother was able to send her electrocardiogram readings effectively to the hospital monitoring her.

563 Brandon wasn't the only inventor in his family. His brother, Spencer, who was three years younger, noticed how, when children in hospitals rode around in toy cars, their IV drips would have to be carried behind by desperate parents. Spencer designed a toy car that incorporated the drip, so the parents wouldn't have to chase around after them.

TOOT TOOT

Bobby takes the newly invented DRIP MOBILE for a test drive. Down the hallway of the hospital at 20 km per hour.

564 The artificial kidney is a lifesaver for people whose own kidneys have failed. It is able to pass blood and clean out chemical waste from the body, just as a normal kidney does. The artificial kidney was invented in 1944 by Willem Kolff.

565 **K**idney transplants began in 1954 when Joseph Murray successfully transplanted a kidney from one twin to the other. Thanks to drugs which can suppress our immune system

and stop it fighting off new implanted tissue, we now don't need a donor to be our twin.

566 **T**he heart-lung machine is a device that replaces the heart's function during surgery. It was invented by John Gibbon Jr in 1953. Over the years vast improvements have been made, but his was the prototype.

567 **T**he polio vaccine was invented by Jonas Salk in 1952 and, like other vaccines, contained the dead virus. The modern form of the polio vaccine was an improved version by Albert Sabin.

568 **D**NA, or deoxyribonucleic acid, is the core of life. Two men, Francis Crick and James Watson, were the ones who discovered the chemical structure of DNA in 1953.

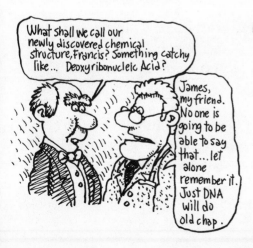

569 **T**he first hip replacement was done in 1962. The operation was performed by John Charnley, who was a British surgeon.

570 The very first heart transplant was done in 1967. The operation was performed by a surgeon from South Africa named Christiaan Barnard.

571 In 1999, Anthony Atala was the first to realise that internal organs could be grown from a single cell. His first successful experiment was a dog's bladder, and it was perfect!

572 Genetic engineering once seemed like it was from the imagination of a science fiction author, but now there have been such major advances in technology that is possible to alter the DNA of an organism. Stanley Cohen and Herbert Boyer discovered the science in 1972.

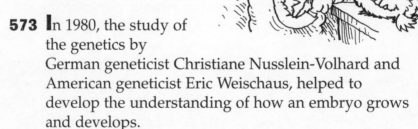

573 In 1980, the study of the genetics by German geneticist Christiane Nusslein-Volhard and American geneticist Eric Weischaus, helped to develop the understanding of how an embryo grows and develops.

574 Gene therapy is a way of replacing faulty genes in sick people. The first person to succeed in removing a faulty gene from a patient was an American named French Anderson, in 1990.

575 The first test-tube baby is named Louise Brown and she was born on 25 July 1978. Using her mother's egg and her father's sperm, the British gynaecologist Patrick Steptoe and colleague Robert Edwards were able to achieve fertilisation outside the womb. The resulting embryo was then placed in the womb, and developed into a healthy child.

576 Prozac® is a drug that can alter the amount of the neurotransmitter serotonin in the brain and thus control depression. Prozac was first approved for use in 1987, and was the first drug of this kind available.

577 The endoscope was invented in 1992. It is able to be pushed into the human body to enable the surgeon to see inside. It works with fibre-optics and a very small camera.

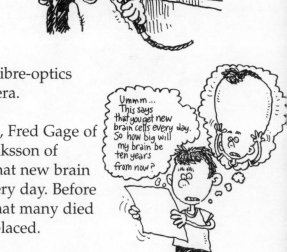

578 In 1998 Two scientists, Fred Gage of America and Peter Eriksson of Sweden, discovered that new brain cells are produced every day. Before this, it was believed that many died daily but were not replaced.

579 The biological molecular motor was invented by Carlo Montemagno of the USA in 1999. The motor, made from a molecule, could pave the way in the future for tiny molecular pumps within the body.

580 British scientist Julia Polak and her team made an important discovery in the medical field. They found that it was possible to grow new bones outside of the human body aided by artificial elements such as bio-glass and silicon.

581 False teeth date back 3000 years to the Etruscans. These ancient people used ivory to replace teeth.

582 French dentists were creating fillings with mercury in the early 1800s. In 1848 Giovanni d'Arcoli suggested gold-leaf fillings, which are still sometimes used today.

583 The first multifunctional dentist chair was patented by Waldo Hanchett in 1848.

584 It wasn't until 1875 that George Green patented the first electric drill for teeth.

585 Cocaine was used as an anaesthetic for dental patients during the late 1800s. Then a German named Alfred Einkorn came up with the idea of using the safer novocain in 1905.

586 The bionic ear, a device that can help some deaf children to hear, is also known as the cochlear implant. Although it was not invented by a single person, it is often attributed to Professor Graeme Clark from Australia, who implanted the first one in 1978.

Mamma mia! I can-a see three doors-a here. Maybe it's-a this-a one.'

BUMP

587 Contact lenses were an idea that had been around since Leonardo Da Vinci's time. However, Adolf Eugen Fick from Germany made the first successful contact lens in 1887.

588 Laser eye surgery was an idea first patented by Dr. Steven Trokel in the 1980s after he was inspired by the delicate nature of a laser that could etch away at a silicone chip. The first eye surgery using lasers was in 1987.

589 Guide dogs were first trained in Germany after the World War One, to aid the soldiers who returned from the war without eyesight. It wasn't long before similar guide dog training schools began in America and England.

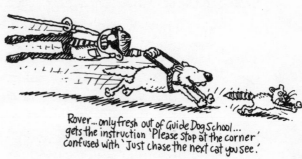

Rover...only fresh out of Guide Dog School... gets the instruction 'Please stop at the corner' confused with 'Just chase the next cat you see.'

Behind the Fiction

Inventions can also be ideas and concepts. Here we look at fifty famous works of the imagination and the inventive minds behind them.

590 *Buffy the Vampire Slayer* – **creator, Joss Whedon (1992 – the original movie)** A simple idea about a high school girl fighting demons that was a huge success!

591 *The X Files* – **creator, Chris Carter (TV series, 1993)** Two FBI agents named Mulder and Scully investigate cases of the paranormal. It was a surprise hit that went from a cult following to a worldwide mainstream TV show.

592 *Star Trek* **(and subsequent spin-offs) – creator, Gene Roddenberry (TV series, 1966)** One of the biggest TV shows of all time, which spawned movies and many TV sequels.

593 *The Simpsons* – **creator, Matt Groening (TV series, 1987)** Originally the cartoon was a space filler between sketches on *The Tracey Ullman Show* but the dysfunctional family soon got its own TV series.

594 *The Chronicles of Narnia* – **author, C. S. Lewis (book, 1950)** A simple tale of four children stumbling across a whole new world through the back of a wardrobe, it captured the imagination of generations.

595 *The Hobbit* **and** *The Lord of the Rings* – **author, J. R. R. Tolkien (books, 1937 & 1954 respectively)** Often voted by critics and the public alike as some of the greatest books ever written.

596 Doctor Who – creator, **Sydney Newman (TV series, 1963)** The longest running science fiction television show of all time. The original series ran for twenty-six years. In 2005, writer and producer Russell T Davies resurrected the series.

597 The Daleks – creator, **Terry Nation (1963)** Many have said that the first season of Doctor Who may not have been as successful if it not for the marvellous creation of the Daleks.

598 The Twilight Zone – creator, **Rod Serling (TV series, 1957, although the first episode aired in 1958)** This horror series still manages to creep people out today with its tight scripts and remarkable performances from various guest stars.

599 Harry Potter series – author, **J.K. Rowling (book, first published in 1997)** The tales of Harry Potter and his friends, Hermione and Ron, have become so firmly rooted in modern pop culture that they are read by children and adults alike.

600 Wallace and Gromit – creator, **Nick Park (TV series, 1989)** A simple inventor and his faithful dog have a series of adventures involving a trip to the moon, a sinister penguin disguised as a chicken, a robotic dog, and a vegetable guzzling were-rabbit.

601 Charlie and the Chocolate Factory – author, **Roald Dahl (book, 1964)** Roald Dahl's most famous story is that of a young boy named Charlie and a factory unlike any seen before.

602 Hercule Poirot and Miss Marple – author, Agatha Christie The first Poirot story, *The Mysterious Affair at Styles* was Agatha's first published novel in 1920. The first Miss Marple story, *The Murder at the Vicarage* was published in 1930.

603 Pokemon – creators, Wizards of the Coast Inc. (computer game, 1996) It all began as a simple computer game but the franchise grew and grew to encapsulate trading cards, a TV series and cuddly toys!

604 T*he Worst Witch* – author, Jill Murphy (book, 1974) Years before Harry Potter was conceived, Jill Murphy had her own version of Hogwarts in Miss Cackle's Academy of Witchcraft.

605 T*he Muppets* – creator, Jim Henson (TV series, as part of 'Sam and Friends', beginning in 1955) The zany humour of Jim Henson and his friend and colleague, Frank Oz, was embraced by television audiences of all ages.

606 M*onty Python's Flying Circus* – creators, John Cleese, Graham Chapman, Eric Idle, Michael Palin, Terry Jones and Terry Gilliam. (TV series, 1969) Perhaps the most popular comedy troupe in television history, these brilliant, hilarious, surreal and occasionally very naughty men changed comedy for ever.

607 A*bsolutely Fabulous* – creators, Jennifer Saunders and Dawn French. (TV series, 1992) The TV series was based on a sketch written by Jennifer Saunders and Dawn French that appeared in their TV series *French and Saunders* back in 1990. Jennifer took the sketch and created one of the biggest comedy hits of the nineties.

608 Artemis Fowl – author, Eoin Colfer (book, 2001) Whoever thought that an anti-hero could gain such a big following? Eoin Colfer's Artemis Fowl is not your regular protagonist, but his diabolical ways have entranced children everywhere.

609 Peanuts (Charlie Brown, Snoopy et al) – cartoonist, **Charles M Schulz (comic strip, 1950)** The stories surrounding Charlie Brown, Lucy, Linus and Snoopy the dog were amusing yet often thought provoking and philosophical.

610 Winnie the Pooh – author, A. A. Milne (book, 1926) The brainchild of A. A. Milne, Pooh Bear and his friends, Piglet, Tigger, Eeyore and others, were charming characters that lived in the Hundred Acre Wood.

611 Alice's Adventures in Wonderland – author, Lewis **Carroll (book, 1865)** Surreal yet enchanting, Alice's adventures had her meeting with some of the strangest characters in literary history, including the Mad Hatter and the Cheshire Cat.

612 Batman – creator, Bob Kane (comic, 1939) Unlike many superheroes, Batman does not actually possess any superhuman powers, but he is aided by some marvellous gadgets and impressive fighting skills.

613 Superman – creators, Jerry **Siegel and Joe Shuster (comic, 1933)** The alien named Kal-El from Krypton fell to Earth as a baby, where he grew up on a farm and found he had superhuman strength and remarkable powers.

614 **W**onder Woman – creator, William Moulton Marston (comic, 1941) Wonder Woman was created as a reaction to the male-dominated comic world. Her adventures began in the pages of DC Comics but eventually became a TV series.

615 **S**piderman – creator, Stan Lee (comic, 1962) A young man is bitten by a radioactive spider and then inherits certain arachnid characteristics.

616 **T**omb Raider/Lara Croft – creators, Eidos Interactive (computer game, 1996) The popular computer game starred the Indiana Jones-inspired Lara Croft and became phenomenally successful, eventually extending the franchise into movies.

617 **T**he Prisoner – creators, Patrick McGoohan and George Markstein (TV series, 1967) A TV series about a secret agent kidnapped and imprisoned by his own people. The prison, known simply as 'The Village', is populated with people all identified by a number. Our hero was Number Six. But who was Number One?

618 **P**eter Rabbit – author, Beatrix Potter (book, 1902) Beatrix Potter told of the simple lives of Peter Rabbit and his friends beautifully. The initial twenty-three books in the series have become timeless classics.

619 **S**am Pig – author, Alison Uttley (book, 1965) Sam was the creation of Alison Uttley but there were a host of other characters, most famously, Brock the Badger.

620 *Thunderbirds* – creators, Sylvia and Gerry Anderson (TV series, 1964) Although the Andersons created several TV series featuring puppets, *Thunderbirds* had the greatest reputation and is still popular today.

621 *The Pink Panther* – creators, Blake Edwards and Maurice Richlin (film, 1963) Initially written for David Niven, the film series took a different turn and starred the bumbling Inspector Clouseau, played to perfection by Peter Sellers.

622 *Gulliver's Travels* – author, Jonathan Swift (book, 1726) One of the most enchanting tales of foreign lands ever penned. Gulliver was famously washed up on the shores of Lilliput where the people were small enough to fit in his palm.

623 *Frankenstein* – author, Mary Shelley (book, 1818) This is a classic story of an inventor named Frankenstein who tried to create life from death through the power of electricity. He unwittingly unleashes his monster!

624 *Dracula* – author, Bram Stoker (book, 1897) Possibly the greatest gothic story ever written, Dracula tells the tale of an ancient vampire and has a darkly romantic plot.

625 *The Adventures of Huckleberry Finn* – author, Mark Twain (book, 1884) This is an American classic about life in the South. Touching and controversial, it captured the hearts of a nation.

626 B_ewitched_ **– creator, Sol Saks (TV series, 1964)** An enchanting sitcom starring Elizabeth Montgomery as Samantha Stevens, a witch married to an ordinary human.

627 T_he Avengers_ **– creator, Sydney Newman (TV series, 1961)** Working for 'The Ministry', Steed was partnered with the likes of Cathy Gale and Emma Peel. They soon became worldwide heroes.

628 T_he Addams Family_ **– cartoonist, Charles Addams (comic strip, 1938)** It began as a comic strip but was eventually made into the TV classic, and then later into a successful movie.

629 T_he Munsters_ **– creator, Allan Burns (TV series, 1964)** Despite obvious comparisons with The Addams Family, this sitcom about a strange collection of Hollywood-style monsters soon earned impressive viewing figures.

630 T_arzan_ **– author, Edgar Rice Burroughs (book, 1914)** Tarzan is one of the most filmed characters in movie history. He was a human who had been raised in the jungle and soon became 'lord of the apes'.

631 T_he Hitchhikers Guide to the Galaxy_ **– author, Douglas Adams (radio series, 1978)** This fabulous piece of science fiction comedy began as a radio series and eventually became a book and then a TV series, before getting the big screen treatment in 2005.

632 T_he Time Machine_ **– author, H.G. Wells (book, 1895)** Time travel has always been a favourite of science fiction authors, but _The Time Machine_ is a masterpiece, with memorable races of the future called the Eloi and the Morlocks.

633 **P***eter Pan* – **author, J.M. Barrie (book, 1902)** The story of a boy who never grew up and the children whose lives he changed.

634 **T***he Jungle Book* – **author, Rudyard Kipling (book, 1894)** A young boy named Mowgli is reared in the jungle by wolves and soon becomes a hero when he defends his animal friends from the dreaded tiger, Shere Kahn.

635 **T***he Canterbury Tales* – **author, Geoffrey Chaucer (book, 1380s–90s)**This is a collection of stories which are narrated by various storytellers competing for a free meal.

636 **J***ames Bond* **series – author, Ian Fleming (book, 1953)** James Bond is an incredibly enduring character who has been at the forefront of popular culture for half a century. Perhaps the literary and movie world's greatest spy!

637 **E**.*T. The Extra-Terrestrial* – **writer, Melissa Mathison and director Steven Spielberg (film, 1982)** An alien is left behind on Earth when his spaceship departs and he befriends a young human boy.

638 **S***py Kids* – **writer & director, Robert Rodriguez (film, 2001)** James Bond for a younger generation, the Spy Kids tackled the biggest enemies of the world with incredible gadgets and witty repartee. Fun for all ages!

639 **T***eenage Mutant Ninja Turtles* – **creators, Kevin Eastman & Peter Laird (comic, 1984)** Four pizza-loving turtles who live in the sewers and come up to street level to fight crime.

A Dedicated Follower of Fashion

640 Trainers or sneakers were a sports shoe designed by Adolf Dasler in 1949, and were very popular with athletes.

Young lady! How can you run in those high heels? You should get yourself some of these newly invented trainers...I can run for kilometres!

I'm only rushing to catch my train.

641 Nike Air Max shoes were introduced in 1987 and boasted an air-cushioned sole. The air pocket can be seen through a small see-through bubble at the side.

642 The zip was originally designed for shoes in 1893 by Whitcomb Judson from Chicago. An engineer from Sweden named Gideon Sundback improved the device by replacing the hooks in the fastener with teeth or cups locking together. The word 'zip' came from the boots on which these fasteners were placed – zippers!

I bought these sandals while on holiday in Mesopotamia. Do you like them?

I do. But I like something up to the knee like these. These were on the half price table in a leather shop in an alley in Crete.

643 The earliest shoes were simply leather sandals. The idea grew and in places like ancient Mesopotamia, feet were covered completely with the leather. Eventually, in Crete, boots were invented that went right up to the knee.

644 Before the invention of shoelaces in the early twentieth century, shoes were often fastened with buckles or buttons. Modern laces are often made of cotton.The small plastic bit on the end is called an 'aglet'.

645 The first underwear to be worn was most likely the loincloth. In the middle ages, men began to wear 'braies', short pantaloons that tied at the waist and above the knee. Women wore an undergarment called a 'shift'.

646 Amelia Bloomer invented bloomers in the mid-nineteenth century. They were similar to trousers, only baggier and with elasticised ankles. Although they originally shocked the world, they would eventually become popular among women.

647 Corsets have been around for just under 4000 years. Around 1900 BC, Minoan men and women in Crete were using tightly bound cloth to squeeze their midriffs into a thin shape.

648 Garters were designed to hold up ladies' stockings before the invention of elastic, and were often decorated in fancy ways with lace and ribbon. These days, garters are often worn by a bride at her wedding.

649 The Mackintosh raincoat was named after its inventor, Charles Macintosh, who was a Scottish chemist. In 1823 he invented waterproof material by binding clothes together with rubber that had been soaked in a substance called coal-tar naphtha.

650 **S**ocks have a mysterious background and little is known about when they first started being worn. It is estimated that it was 2000–3000 years ago.

651 **L**ong johns are a style of thermal underwear that, until recent times, was often worn by men in North America when it was very cold. They were either a two-piece or, in some cases, an all-in-one that was also known as a 'union suit'. The two piece suits are still in use to this day.

652 **G**loves were not always worn to keep people's hands warm in cold weather. Often, as with many garments, they were of ceremonial value. Gloves were discovered in the tomb of King Tutankhamen in Egypt.

653 **J**acob Davis and Levi Strauss invented denim jeans during the gold rush of the 1840s and 50s, in America. They patented their idea in 1873 and it has now remained a staple in fashion, decade after decade.

654 **S**ilk, from the silk worm, was discovered by the Chinese over 4500 years ago. It was one of the best-kept secrets in the fashion world for centuries!

655 **A**rtificial silk wasn't invented until around 1884, when both Joseph Swan and Hilaire Chardonnet individually came up with an idea for making a substitute silk from a cellulose nitrate chemical solution.

656 **A** new artificial material called viscose rayon was invented by Charles Cross, Clayton Beadle and Edward Bevan in 1892, as a safer alternative to the flammable artificial silk.

657 **K**imonos are a traditional garments worn by the Japanese. Dating from around 700 AD, they are renowned for their elegance and complex designs, which can be works of art in themselves. Kimonos are still worn today but mostly only on special occasions.

658 **L**ycra® or spandex was invented in 1959 by the Du Pont Chemical company. It is widely used in garments for sports men and women.

659 **N**ylon was invented by Wallace Carothers in 1935, during the search for a substitute to silk. Originally used for washing lines and toothbrushes, nylon proved suitable for clothing and pantyhose/tights.

660 Polyester is a synthetic fibre discovered by John Rex Whinfield, James Tennant, W. K. Birtwhistle and C. G. Ritchie in 1941 in the UK. It is made from the chemical polyethylene terephthalate.

661 Some T-shirts in the 1980s were treated with thermochromatic dyes that made the T-shirt change colour with heat. This invention came from the company named Global Hypercolour.

662 Velcro® was invented by Switzerland's George de Mestral in 1955. He was fascinated by some burrs that had clung to his dog's fur. After analysing the burrs under a microscope, he came up with a new way of fastening clothes.

663 Buttonholes weren't invented until the beginning of the thirteenth century, even though buttons had been around centuries before this. The old-style buttons had been held by loops. Now, the holes within the clothes made it possible to fasten them in a more practical way.

JULIA'S MUM FINDS ANOTHER USE FOR VELCRO

664 The history of elastic begins with rubber, from the sap of the rubber tree. In 1820, English inventor Thomas Hancock created a machine called the masticator, which shredded and recycled rubber. From there he was able to develop elastic fabrics and thin strips to sew inside garments.

665 An American named Walter Hunt, who specialised in mechanics, designed the safety pin in its modern form. However, around 250 BC a similar device was worn by the Romans and the Greeks as a way of keeping their robes from falling open.

BRUTUS COPS FLAK FROM THE LOCAL REBELS ABOUT HIS SAFETY PIN.

Hey Brutus! Is that a safety pin off a baby's nappy holding your cape on?

666 Vinyl is a type of polymer and is often a substitute for leather. It is known for its inability to 'breathe', so it is not always as comfortable as wearing leather and was invented in 1926 by Amercian researcher Waldo Lonsbury Semon.

667 Knitting is a very useful way of making clothes from fibres, and it is likely that one of the first peoples to knit without the aid of a loom were the nomads who roamed North America 3000 years ago.

668 The knitting machine was an invention that came from a clergyman named William Lee. In 1589, he designed a machine that would knit in a loom-type fashion and was much faster than hand-knitting.

Well... it's different! Marcus will be the only Centurion on Hadrian's Wall with a cape like this!

Lucilla gets a little carried away with her newly invented pair of Roman scissors while working on a cape for her husband Marcus Trebius.

669 Material for clothing often needed to be cut, and the Romans invented scissors around 100 AD. Other cutting devices had been around for thousands of years, but the Romans' was the pivoted design we know so well today.

670 In 1733, John Kay invented the flying shuttle. This object was a wheeled device on a track that would zoom back and forth within a loom and speed up the process of weaving.

671 The spinning jenny was advancement on the spinning wheel, as it could spin more than one thread at a time. James Hargreaves built it in 1764.

672 In 1769, the process of making thread for weaving was improved upon by Richard Arkwright from England. His spinning machine was powered by water.

673 A year later, Mr Arkwright put the classic waterwheel and his water-powered spinning wheel to work in the same building. This was in Cromford in Derbyshire, England. It became the world's first factory!

674 In 1785, Edmund Arkwright, a parson from England, invented the power loom. A couple of years later he would have a factory of his own. The late eighteenth century and the early nineteenth century was the beginning of Britain's Industrial Revolution.

675 The cotton gin was a device that can remove the seeds of the cotton plant and retrieve the cotton fibre freely. Eli Whitney invented it in 1793.

676 A further refinement of the loom came about in 1801. Jacques de Vaucanson and Joseph-Marie Jacquard conceived and developed a punch-card system that instructed the loom to alter the pattern of the threads to create different patterns.

677 In the early days, lace was made by hand. It was such a delicate craft that it was very expensive. In 1809, John Heathcote from England invented a machine that could copy the process and make lace much faster.

678 American inventors Walter Hunt and Elias Howe developed the concept of sewing machines in 1843 and 1846 respectively. However, it was Isaac Singer who perfected the home sewing machine, and his name is associated with the product today.

679 Lipstick has been a part of the fashion world for as long as make-up has, but it was Maurice Levy in 1915 who revolutionised the accessory by placing it in a tube for portable use.

680 Cecil Gee, a tailor, designed the first buttoned shirt in 1932 due to public demand, as people were tired of pulling garments on over their heads!

681 The bikini was invented in 1946 by two rival fashion designers in France. They both came up with the two-piece swimsuit for women. One, designed by Jacques Heim, was called the Atome and the other, designed by Louis Reard, was called the Bikini.

682 The clothes mannequin has been around for well over 100 years and has been made from wood and plastics. Nobody is entirely sure who made the very first model.

683 False eyelashes were not a product originally intended for the public. They were made for the film studios so that female lead actors' eyelashes would stand out. Designed in 1947 by David and Eric Alyott from Britain, they soon became popular with women in general.

684 Miniskirts were enormously popular in the liberated 1960s. They were designed by a French designer called André Courreges in 1964.

THE MINISKIRT

685 Nail polishing has been around for centuries. The Chinese were making colourings from beeswax and gum 5000 years ago. The ancient Egyptians used henna to dye their nails.

Adjedaa...my faithful nail technician. What colours do you have for my nails today?

We have Desert Brown... Brown River... Henna Brown ...Brown Sunset... Brown Sunrise ...Sky Brown... Plain Brown... Dung Brown and Beetle Brown. Basically...all we have is brown, my Queen of the Nile.

Florence... You've just had your hair coloured with that new invention... hair dye.

Does it come in any other colour than green?

686 The first artificial hair dye was an invention by Eugene Schueller (the founder of L'Oreal) in 1907. Natural substances such as henna had been previously used.

687 For many years people tried to disguise their body odour (unsatisfactorily) with perfumes and colognes. In 1888 a gentleman in Philadelphia made the first antiperspirant that would prevent underarm odour. It was the beginning of the product known as Mum®.

688 The young Max Factor was fascinated by concoctions and potions while he was an apprentice for a pharmacist. In due course, he opened a shop in Moscow selling make-up products and eventually moved to America in 1908. His products have gone on to be incredibly famous.

689 The first machine to create 'permanent' curled hair (or perm) was devised by Charles Nestle at the turn of the twentieth century.

690 Although Mary Phelps Jacob invented the first brassiere, it was the famous film director Howard Hughes who designed the cantilevered, steel-rimmed bra for the film star Jane Russell in 1941.

Albert Parkhouse... coathanger designer... experiments until he finds the right shape.

691 The wire coat hanger was invented by Albert J. Parkhouse in 1903 when he heard colleagues complain about the coat hooks at the Timberlake Wire and Novelty Company in the United States.

692 Perfume has been around for thousands of years. The earliest dates back to the ancient Egyptians, who often used it in religious ceremonies.

693 Wigs have been around for a long time. Ancient Egyptians wore wigs for decorative purposes. They were often made of human hair attached to a net.

694 Watches were not originally designed as fashion items, but as a portable way to tell the time. Peter Henlein from Germany invented the first pocket watch in 1524, and it was as large as a fist. Over time, watches became smaller and various designs made them a fashion accessory – right up to the present day where we now wear them on our wrists!

Eat Me, Drink Me!

695 Champagne is named after the region in France where it is made. It has been suggested that the first person to make this type of bubbly wine was the winemaker Dom Perignon, in 1670.

DOM PERIGNON NEARLY DOESN'T INVENT CHAMPAGNE IN 1670

696 The corkscrew was invented around the same time as the use of corks to seal bottled wine in the late 1600s. It is said that the first corkscrews were tools with a spiral end, usually used for cleaning out the end of a musket gun!

697 The wine cask box was invented in Australia. The wine is kept preserved in a vacuum-sealed foil bag and is released through a nozzle. Tom Angove, a wine maker from South Australia, came up with the idea and patented it in 1965.

698 Condensed milk is made through the process of heating and sterilising milk without it losing the flavour. Gail Borden came up with this idea in 1856 to store milk longer.

699 The first milking machine was a vacuum-like device that could draw the milk from a cow's udder. It was designed in 1860 by L. O. Colvin.

700 **M**argarine was an award-winning invention by Hippolyte Mege-Mouries of France in 1869. The first margarine contained ingredients such as pig's stomachs and cows' udders. It was very popular, and its original name was 'Butterine'.

701 **S**accharin was discovered in 1879 when two chemists named Constantin Fahlberg and Ira Remsen wondered why everything in their lab tasted sweet. They soon realised it was due to saccharin, so they decided to sell it as an artificial sweetener.

702 **T**he Coca-Cola® company was founded by the drinks inventor John Pemberton, in 1892. Coca-Cola® was originally so named because it contained cocaine and caffeine (which came from kola-nuts). The drink no longer contains cocaine.

703 **S**oup is 8000 years old. The word originally comes from the term to describe bread that has been soaked in meat juices – 'sop'.

704 **A** German housewife named Melitta Bentz invented the coffee filter in 1908 when seeking a way to prevent over-brewing coffee. Her invention enabled hot water to pass through the coffee and soak up the flavour.

705 Instant coffee was invented in 1901 by a Japanese-American named Satori Kato.

706 Although the very first espresso machine was made in France in 1822, it wasn't until 1938 that the Italian Achilles Gaggia created a machine with a high-pressure system, producing an espresso by forcing water through the beans.

The invention of the TV DINNER in 1954 was great for Irving. It meant he could pile up enough food to last him a whole week in front of the television without moving.

Gee I hope somebody can invent a TV remote control to change the channel. I can't move for all of this food!

707 Thanks to the invention of the television, Gerry Thomas invented the TV dinner in 1954. In post-war America there was a trend to try and limit domestic work and increase leisure time, so the TV dinner was warmly welcomed. Presented in metal trays, they were easily heated and contained all the necessary requirements for a meal.

Friends...Romans... countrymen...and everybody else for that matter. I...Julius Caesar would like you to think I invented CAESAR SALAD....

but I didn't! It was some Mexican guy.

708 Caesar salad was not invented by the great Julius Caesar, but rather by a Mexican named Caesar Gardini in the 1920s.

709 Chocolate was first used by the Olmec Indians, the Mayans and the Aztecs. It was a drink made from the cocoa bean. The Aztecs called it 'xocalatl', which is the link to the modern word, 'chocolate'. This translates to 'warm and bitter liquid'.

710 The first chocolate bar was made by Joseph Fry & Son in 1847.

711 A man named Frank Mars invented the Milky Way, a chocolate bar with a soft nougat filling, in 1922.

712 Forrest Mars invented the Mars Bar in 1932, when he moved to England from the US after an argument with his father.

713 The first official commercial production of lemonade was in Paris, France, in 1676 by a company named Compagnie de Limonadiers. At this early stage, lemonade was not carbonated, so it did not have bubbles.

714 Joseph Priestley initiated fizzy drinks in 1772, after the naturally carbonated water found in springs inspired him.

WILLIAM SHAKES THE FIRST FIZZY DRINK IN 1772.

715 Plastic bottles which can contain the pressure of fizzy drinks were invented in 1973 by Nathaniel Wyeth when he used the plastic polyethylene terephthalate. Stretching the plastic during the moulding process strengthened the bottle.

716 Vitamins were an important discovery. Frederick Hopkins from England worked out that we needed more than just the carbohydrates, fats and proteins in our diet and identified there was something else important in food. In 1912, a biochemist from Poland named Casimir Funk decided to call these bonus ingredients 'vitamines' after the amine found in rice.

717 Pizza has been around for centuries but the first pizza shop was opened in Naples, in 1830. This shop is still selling pizzas today!

718 The circular stand that sometimes comes in the pizza box to prevent the lid getting squashed onto the topping was invented by Carmela Vitale from New York in 1983.

719 It has been suggested that ice-cream has been around from as early as the time of Emperor Nero in the Roman period – around 37 AD.

720 The hamburger has its origins in Germany. When German immigrants went to the USA, they took their concept of meat patties in a sandwich or roll with them.

Oh look, Otto! That little dog looks so hot... and he looks just like that sausage on that bread roll you're eating. He must be a hot dog!

Oh Hilda... You've made me dribble sauce on my trousers!

721 Hot dogs were also from Germany. Germans are renowned for their various sausages and it was easier to eat them when wrapped in a blanket of bread or a roll. It is suspected that the term 'hot dog' comes from the similarity of the sausage to a Dachshund 'sausage' dog.

I've eaten so many of these I think they need to name them after me!

So you want to call it... The Earl?

No, you fool! The Sandwich!

THE EARL OF SANDWICH HAS AN IDEA IN BETWEEN MOUTHFULS.

722 The sandwich is named after the Earl of Sandwich, who invented it in the middle of the eighteenth century. He was extremely fond of eating meat placed between two slices of toast.

723 The history of the Cornish pasty is embedded in folklore, but the tale of fishermen's wives making their husbands' lunch and wrapping it in pastry certainly provides a reasonable answer to the mystery.

724 In 1962, a Canadian named Edward Asselbergs dehydrated potato flakes in order to make instant mashed potato.

725 Tomato ketchup was first made by the Heinz Company in 1876. The word 'ketchup' comes from a Chinese word 'ke-tsiap', which is a type of pickled fish dressing.

726 Mayonnaise dates as far back as the mid-eighteenth century in France when the Duke De Richelieu's chef made it. It was named in celebration of the Duke's win over the British in the battle at Port Mahon – 'Mahonnaise'!

727 Jell-O® or jelly appeared in 1845, when Peter Cooper patented a gelatin dessert. Despite this, he never manufactured it and later Pearle B. Wait bought the patent from him. He and his wife May also failed to storm the marketplace and the patent was bought once again by Frank Woodward. After a few false starts, his company succeeded in bringing jelly to the masses.

728 Forrest Mars created M&Ms inspired by the soldiers in the Spanish Civil War, who were eating sugar-coated lumps of chocolate.

729 Pez was originally intended as a cigarette substitute! In 1927, an Austrian named Eduard Haas invented them, and the first Pez were peppermint flavoured.

730 The idea of freeze-drying foods comes from the ancient Peruvian Inca society. However, for western culture, freeze-drying was introduced in World War Two, when the process was developed to transport and preserve blood plasma!

731 Coffee dates back to about 800 BC, but it is likely it was being drunk for a long time before then. Surprisingly, the western world has only been drinking it for about three hundred years.

732 The doughnut/donut with a hole was invented by Captain Hanson Crockett Gregory in the 1840s, but it was William Rosenberg who opened up the first 'Dunkin' Donut' chain in 1948 in the USA.

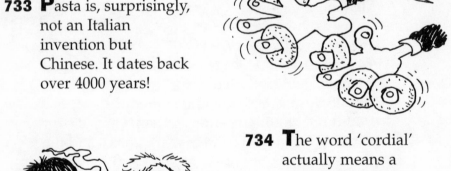

733 Pasta is, surprisingly, not an Italian invention but Chinese. It dates back over 4000 years!

734 The word 'cordial' actually means a sweet spirit made from berries. The spirit is more widely known as a liqueur these days. Cordial is now used in reference to a child's squash drink.

735 Pretzels are fifteen centuries old and have been a popular snack for fasting Christians and Jews, as the ingredients are merely flour and water. It is said the form of the pretzel represents the holy trinity.

736 Sushi is a Japanese invention and although most believe the term relates to the raw fish, it actually refers to the use of sushi rice (seasoned with vinegar).

737 The pavlova is a meringue dessert and was named after the ballerina Anna Matveyevna Pavlova. It is hotly debated between Australia and New Zealand as to which country originally invented it during her tour of the two countries in 1926.

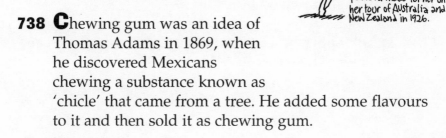

Geev me more orv thart luvorly pavlova darlink!

Anna samples every pavlova made for her on her tour of Australia and New Zealand in 1926.

738 Chewing gum was an idea of Thomas Adams in 1869, when he discovered Mexicans chewing a substance known as 'chicle' that came from a tree. He added some flavours to it and then sold it as chewing gum.

739 Bubblegum was invented in 1928 by Walter Diemer, when he was working at a chewing gum factory.

PPFFFFF PPFFFFF PFFFF

OK...OK! Now what do I do with a bubblegum bubble that's bigger than me? If this goes KABOOM... I'm a goner!

740 **C**heesecake originated in ancient Greece and was a staple food of the athletes in the Olympics!

Would you care for another piece of cheesecake before you head out for your 5000 metres semi final Dimitri?

Oh! Could I have ice cream or cream with it, please?

A SCENE AT THE WARM-UP TRACK AT THE ANCIENT OLYMPICS.

741 **W**ill Keith Kellogg invented corn flakes in 1894 when he was researching a healthy diet for hospital patients.

742 **C**ereals in general were created by the members of the American Seventh-Day Adventists, who made and sold cereal in 1860.

743 **A** weird invention from the Nabisco Company in the United States was cheese in a can. This is real cheese that can be sprayed from a nozzle.

744 **F**rank Epperson invented the ice lolly or popsicle, and he patented the idea in 1924.

Oh my! I'm sure one of those genetically engineered tomatoes just growled at me!

GGRRRR

I wasn't growling. It was indigestion.

745 **A**n American company named Calgene Inc. produced the first genetically engineered tomato called the FlavrSavr® in 1992. It was more flavoursome than previous varieties.

746 **T**he Esky® is a type of carrier that keeps food and drinks cool. It was designed by the Nylex company in Australia and introduced in 1952.

It's a Mad, Mad World

747 In 1995, the Alarm Fork was invented. The idea was that you could only eat when the fork's light was green, thus reducing the amount and speed of eating.

Great! A fork at one end and chopsticks at the other end. So how do I eat my soup?

748 **P**atent Number: US3984595 Donald Stephens of New York invented a rug that could be inflated into a mattress for when guests stay overnight.

749 **P**atent Number: US4809435 Gerald Printz designed an eating utensil that from one end looked like a pair of chopsticks, but at the other was a fork.

750 **P**atent Number: US5934226 Mark and Lorraine Moore invented a bird diaper/nappy which, when attached to a pet bird, caught any droppings as it flew about the house.

AAAARKK

Here I am... a 45-year-old parrot and I fly around the house with a nappy on... How ridiculous!

751 **P**atent Number: US6351867 Gerard Foster invented a body squeegee that was a glove with a rubber band attached, and was used to dry oneself without a towel.

752 Patent Number: US5830035 David Budreck in the USA designed a toe puppet. It was a puppet that can be attached to your toe. Why? No idea!

753 Patent Number: US5213428 Nasar Salman invented the biodegradable toothbrush which fits snugly over the finger and can be disposed of in an environmentally friendly way.

754 Patent Number: US5971829 Richard Hartman of Issaquah, in the USA, invented the motorised ice-cream cone, which rotated the product while it was being eaten.

755 Patent Number: US5443036 Martin Abbott and Kevin Amiss designed a product to exercise your cat. It is a hand-held apparatus with an invisible light which the cat will chase, and run off excess fat. Either do that, or just use a torch!

756 Patent Number: US5131832 Chad Budreau combined the cigarette lighter and the ice-cream scoop to make a heated scoop to dig into frozen solid ice-cream.

Buddy is just so taken by the new heated ice cream scoop ...he just can't stop scooping.

SANTA GETS SPRUNG AT 2·30 AM BY THE SANTA DETECTOR.

AARKK
AARKK
AARKK
AARKK

757 Patent Number: US5523741 Thomas Cane from California, USA, has invented a Santa Claus detector. This device is part of a stocking and will light up when activated by an approaching gift-giver.

758 Patent Number: US4887543 Sondra Rockhill from New Jersey, USA, invented a device which, when unclipped from an umbrella, will alert you if you leave the umbrella behind somewhere, making sure you never lose it.

759 Patent Number: US5307162 It sounds like science fiction, but is it? Richard Schowengerdt from California, USA, has

TICK
TICK
TICK

THERE'S A GOLD WATCH IN THIS CIRCLE, BUT THERE'S A CLOAKING DEVICE BEING USED SO YOU CAN'T SEE IT.

patented a cloaking device that uses optoelectronics that can shield an object, giving the illusion that the object isn't there at all.

760 Patent Number: US4805654 Kuo-Hsin Wang from Taiwan has patented a design for a sun-shield for a car that acts as an umbrella, protecting the car from harmful sun rays.

761 **P**atent Number: US5571247 In the event of being attacked by killer bees, it is recommended you jump into this device patented by Virginia Butler from California, USA. That is, if you have one! This cylindrical container fits a human being and is made from polythene and nylon, making it possible to breathe inside, and escape the angry bees.

762 **P**atent Number: US4150505 Kill two birds with one stone? And while you're at it, get the cat fed. This device can catch and kill a bird such as a sparrow, and then deliver it to your cat – that is, if your cat is too lazy to do it himself.

763 **P**atent Number: US5457821 The invention we have all been waiting for! How did we manage for thousands of years without it? This invention is a baseball cap with a wide white rim and a yellow dome over the crown. It gives the impression that the wearer has a giant fried egg on their head. Genius!

764 **P**atent Number: US5713081 This invention is truly amazing. It is a design for pantyhose with a third leg... just in case you have one!

A Mixed Bag of Science

765 The first robot was invented around 370 BC! Archytas of Tarentum, Greece, was a scientist who fashioned a pigeon out of wood. His wooden robot bird moved like a flying bird when rotated on a steam-powered arm.

766 Clocks have come in many forms, from the sundial to the digital, but the first mechanical clock was designed by Su Sung in 1088. It was a waterwheel that would repeatedly fill a bucket of water and then empty it in a steady clockwork fashion.

767 Three hundred years later, Henry de Vick of France made the first official clockwork clock. However, this was not as accurate as Su Sung's.

DANG
DANG
DANG

Oh-a boy!
Like-a I don't-a
know it's-a three
o'clock. This clock-a
tell-a me-a what-a time
it is-a every hour!

768 In 1335, the first chiming clock was created in Milan in Italy. It would sound every hour.

DUTCHMAN CHRISTIAN HUYGENS FAILS TO KEEP HIS OWN EYES ON HIS PENDULUM WHILE DEMONSTRATING THE WORKINGS OF HIS NEW CLOCK TO FRIENDS IN 1657.

Now, my friends. Keep your eye on the heavy pendulum swinging back and forth... back and forth back and forth. That is what keeps my clock...

CLUNK

769 In 1657, Dutchman Christian Huygens applied Galileo's theory of marking off time through a pendulum. He created a clock that had improved function.

770 In 1955, Louis Essen and Jack Parry invented the most accurate timepiece in the world, known as the atomic clock. It is so delicate it can sense the vibration of atoms.

771 The Hamilton Watch Company made a prototype pulsar digital watch in 1970. Two years later it was on the market, with a light-emitting diode display.

What do you think of my new space age watch with a light-emitting diode display?

But it's got no hands! How are you going to tell the time?

1970s THINKING!

772 The barometer, named in 1676 by Edme Mariotte, was invented by a friend of Galileo's called Evangelista Torricelli. Mercury within a calibrated tube rose and fell depending on the air pressure outside.

773 Mercury was also used in the thermometer, which worked on a similar principle. In 1714, Daniel Fahrenheit realised mercury would expand in high temperatures. He applied this to his own thermometer, then named the scale of heat after himself.

774 The Celsius scale was invented by Anders Celsius in 1742 when he was frustrated with the oddly placed numbers in the Fahrenheit scale. He preferred to go decimal but, strangely, decided to make 100 degrees the freezing point and 0 the boiling point. This was eventually inverted.

775 Porcelain is a fine yet strong type of pottery, and is made when the ingredients are heated to a point where they become glasslike. The Chinese were behind its creation around 800 AD.

776 Photography had its beginnings in 1826 when Nicephore Niepce from France placed a sheet of metal coated in tar into a box with a glass lens window in one side. After a few hours, the sunlight had penetrated the lens and left an image on the tarred metal, producing the first photograph!

777 In 1851, Frederick Archer improved the photographic system by painting glass with a cellulose liquid. This acted as a negative and produced better quality pictures. They became known as 'wet-plates'.

778 **A** British man called Richard Maddox designed the 'dry-plates' for photography in 1871. These used gelatine instead of the cellulose liquid.

779 **I**n 1888, an American businessman named George Eastman founded the Kodak Camera Company. The cameras came with film inside them and when you had finished the roll, you returned the camera to the company, which would develop the film for you.

780 **G**eorge Eastman was sold a different type of photographic paper that could be developed in artificial light instead of just daylight. A Belgian named Leo Baekeland invented it in 1891.

781 **B**lack and white pictures were printed using a process called 'half-tone', which was invented by Max and Louis Levy in 1890.

782 **T**he Lumière brothers invented colour photography in 1907, using an autochrome process. They used three colour plates – red, green and blue – which they combined to form a colour picture.

783 Colour film was finally perfected in 1935 by Leopold Mannes and Leopold Godowsky. It was used by Kodak, and called was Kodachrome®.

784 The 35-millimetre camera was designed by Oskar Barnack in 1924 and was an adaptation of the 35mm movie film.

785 The first examples of holography (3D projections) were created in 1948, and were a brainwave of Dennis Gabor from Hungary. Interestingly, his concept came before the invention of the laser, which is the tool used to make holograms these days.

786 In 1931, Harold Edgerton created the flash for a camera by using xenon gas and a high voltage pulse.

787 The idea of Polaroid® sunglasses was developed by Edwin Land in 1929. Polaroid lenses allow through only light that comes from one direction, excluding light from other directions (for example, light bouncing off water). This makes images clearer to the eye.

788 Edwin Land went on to invent the black and white Polaroid® camera in 1947, which could develop a piece of film within sixty seconds.

789 The colour Polaroid camera was, once again, an invention of Edwin Land in the 1950s. He called it Polacolor, and it had three layers of film sensitive to different tones – red, green and blue. Once more, the developing process took a mere sixty seconds.

790 LASER stands for light amplification by simulated emission of radiation. The concept was discovered in 1958 by two physicists, Charles Townes and Arthur Schawlow.

GLUTIUS MAXIMUS ARRIVES HOME IN ROME AFTER FIVE YEARS IN GAUL FIGHTING THE BARBARIANS.

791 The ruby laser was the first real example of a working laser. It was created by an American, Theodore Maiman, in 1960.

792 Streetlamps were first invented by the Romans in 50 AD. The lamps were not very bright, as they were only fuelled by oil.

793 **L**ater, in 1807, Humphry Davy discovered how to make arc light though electricity. However, this type of electric streetlight would not be used until 1883.

794 **H**umphry Davy also invented the Davy lamp, used by miners. Before its invention, miner's lamps with a flame were dangerous, as the methane gas from underground was flammable and caused many explosions. Davy and George Stevenson both came up with similar lamps that were much safer to operate in the mines.

795 **A**nother life-saving mining invention was the safety fuse. In 1831, William Bickford made a cloth that bound gunpowder and would burn slowly, giving miners enough time to light it and then get away before the explosion.

796 **S**wedish man Alfred Nobel invented dynamite in 1867. His fame and fortune led him to institute the annual award of the Nobel Prize.

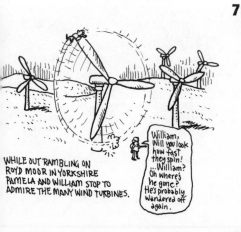

WHILE OUT RAMBLING ON ROYD MOOR IN YORKSHIRE PAMELA AND WILLIAM STOP TO ADMIRE THE MANY WIND TURBINES.

William, will you look how fast they spin! ...William? Oh where's he gone? He's probably wandered off again.

797 **T**he windmill was an extension of the waterwheel in many respects. Wind drove the windmill's sails, which drove a millstone to grind wheat and corn. Even though windmills were around in 600 AD, they remain useful up to the present day, when they can now generate electricity.

798 The first windmill that was able to rotate depending on the direction of the wind was blowing was a towering contraption built in the early part of the fifteenth century.

799 The Chinese were the first people to discover gunpowder over a thousand years ago by mixing three ingredients together to make an explosive. Originally intended for amusement and fireworks, gunpowder would also be used for military purposes.

Wing Sei discovers which three magic compounds make gunpowder the hard way.

800 Fireworks became popular forms of amusement around 1000 years ago and at the time could only burn yellow. Eight hundred years later, they would be able to burn various colours thanks to a French chemist named Claude Berthollet.

801 The microscope is an instrument that combines lenses together in order to magnify the smallest object. Hans Janssen was the first to attempt to make a microscope, in 1600 in Holland.

Hans, my good friend. That is the most awful thing in all of Holland... Did you find it at the bottom of a dyke?

No, Pieter. That's just one of those ants walking around the table.

802 The modern version of the microscope uses a condenser to illuminate the object under view. This was invented by Ernst Able around 1870.

803 In 1942, a microscope with an even greater magnification was invented by Vladimir Zworykin and it was known as the SEM, scanning electron microscope.

804 A field ion microscope can see atoms. The field ion microscope was invented by Erwin Muller from Germany in 1956.

805 In 1981, Gerd Binning and Heinrich Rohrer invented an incredibly powerful microscope capable of seeing the three-dimensional qualities of the atom. It is known as a scanning tunnelling microscope.

806 Alessandro Volta from Italy invented the first battery in 1800, using silver and zinc. His invention was inspired by his friend Luigi Galvini, who had noticed a dead frog's muscles would spasm when in contact with two different metals.

No one's poking me with bits of metal!

AFTER BEING POKED WITH TWO PIECES OF METAL TO TEST MUSCLE SPASM BY LUIGI GALVANI, A DEAD FROG DECIDES ITS NOT DEAD AFTER ALL AND HOPS AWAY.

807 The lead-acid battery still in use in cars today was invented by the Frenchman Gaston Plante, in 1859.

If Mr Gaston Plante is the guy that invented lead acid car batteries, he can come back and get this one... because it's flat! And while he's at it... he can give me a lift because I am now late for work!

808 The first calculator was simply called an adding machine, and was designed by Thomas de Colmar in 1820. Sadly, because he was an insurance man and not an engineer, it didn't work to the standard he desired. Other inventors would make improvements to it over the next thirty years.

809 In 1885, William Burroughs invented the adder-lister, which printed out the calculations it made.

AN ACCOUNTANT'S WORST NIGHTMARE IN 1885.

810 The comptometer was designed in 1887 by Dorr E. Felt and was in competition with Burroughs' machine. Although Felt's machine did not print, it was ultimately quicker.

811 Aluminium was discovered by a chemist named Christian Orsted in 1825 when he extracted it from aluminium chloride.

812 The match in its current form was invented in 1827 by a British chemist named John Walker. Through friction, a phosphorus-tipped stick would ignite and create flames.

813 The water turbine was invented in 1827 by Benoit Fourneyron. It had the power of six horses! Eventually Fourneyron designed turbines that made electricity.

814 Englishman Michael Faraday discovered in 1831 that magnetism could produce electricity. An American named Joseph Henry discovered it at a similar time, but Faraday's notes were published first.

MICHAEL FARADAY TRIES TO ESTABLISH A LINK BETWEEN MAGNETISM AND ELECTRICITY.

815 Eduard Simon from Germany invented polystyrene in 1839 but it was prone to crumbling. An improvement came in 1937 when Robert Dreisbach from America made it more durable.

816 The word 'gyroscope' describes an instrument that is a spinning wheel mounted inside a ring. The gyroscope is a useful navigation instrument, especially for aeroplanes. Jean Foucault designed the gyroscope in 1852 to imitate the Earth spinning on its axis.

817 A Russian named Dmitry Mendeleyev compiled the periodic table in 1869. This covered all the elements and listed them in order of their atomic weight.

818 Plastic in its earliest successful form was called celluloid. John Hyatt invented this in 1870. However, it was rather flammable and refinements were eventually made.

819 Two men trying to make textured wallpaper invented bubble wrap. Marc Chavannes and Alfred Fielding designed the air-pocketed wrapping in 1960.

820 In 1873, Joseph Glidden from the USA made a machine that could churn out miles of barbed wire. Barbed wire was then widely used in the farming community, and it still is, all around the world today.

821 Alexander Graham Bell not only invented the telephone, he also invented the first metal detector. It was 1881 and the President James Garfield had been shot. Bell hurriedly made a device to find the bullet.

822 The improved and portable metal detector was designed by Gerhard Fischar in 1925.

823 James Dewar was the first man to turn oxygen into a liquid by freezing it. His only problem was keeping it safe, so he invented the Dewer vacuum flask in 1892, which was made of reflective glass.

824 The Thermos® flask, very similar to Dewer's design, was more durable for everyday use. Instead of being made of glass all over, the inner bottle was glass and the outer surface was metal. The name 'thermos' was the result of a competition!

825 At the turn of the twentieth century, Francis Galton and Edward Henry invented fingerprinting. They found that every fingerprint is completely different and also worked on a way of classifying the patterns. This brilliant use of evidence was first used in a courtroom in 1902.

826 DNA fingerprinting would come much later, in 1984. Just like a fingerprint, each person's DNA is totally individual. Alec Jeffreys from Britain invented the system which is now in widespread use.

827 The lie detector was created in 1904 by Max Wertheimer. This machine would register heartbeat, blood pressure and breathing patterns, and enabled an operator to tell if someone was lying or not. A much more advanced machine called the polygraph was invented by John Larson in 1921.

828 The neon sign was an invention by Frenchman Georges Claude in 1902, who lit the neon gas within a glass tube with electricity.

829 The particle accelerator was invented in 1932 by John Cockcroft and Ernest Walton, in order to study protons and other sub-atomic particles.

830 Perspex®, a thick plastic, was first sold in 1934. It was invented by Rowland Hill and John Crawford after being inspired by the plexiglas they had seen made by German, Otto Rohm.

831 Eric Fawcett and Reginald Gibson invented another type of plastic called polyethylene in 1935, whilst experimenting with ethylene gas.

832 Polypropylene is a very tough form of plastic that you will recognise from durable dustbins outside the home. It was invented by Karl Ziegler and Giulio Natta in 1954.

833 RADAR (radio detection and ranging) was invented by Robert Watson-Watt in 1935 as a way of detecting enemy aircraft.

834 An insecticide called DDT was invented by Paul Muller in 1939 and was, for a while, sprayed on many crops and even soldiers during World War II. It is not used any longer as it is quite poisonous.

835 The Richter scale is a way of measuring seismic tremors and earthquakes. It was invented by Charles Richter and Beno Gutenberg in 1935.

836 In 1939, scientists discovered that atoms could be split through a process called nuclear fission. This would lead to the development of the atomic bomb. It was soon realised how dangerous this discovery could be in the wrong hands.

837 The first nuclear reactor was created inside a squash court in a university in Chicago by Enrico Fermi in 1942.

838 The first synthetic diamonds were created in 1955 by Percy Bridgman of the General Electric Company by applying high pressure to the material diamond is made of, carbon. Diamond is the hardest material on Earth, so these diamonds are used for cutting tools and drills.

839 In 1941, an American scientist named Russell Ohl discovered the wonders of solar power while working with impure silicon.

840 Willard Libby invented carbon dating in 1947 as a means of discovering how old objects are. He realised that a radioactive form of carbon, carbon-14, decays at a certain rate and, depending on its state of decay, you can estimate how old an object is.

841 **K**nown simply as ANN, the artificial neural network was designed in 1960 by Frank Rosenblatt. It helps us understand how the neural paths of the living brain actually work.

842 **T**he world of science needed a system of measurements that everyone could use so as not to complicate matters. A system known as the Systeme Internationale d'Unites (or 'SI' for short) was implemented by the eleventh General Conference on Weights and Measures in 1960.

843 **T**here are metal alloys (combinations of metals) that have a memory of the shape they were in when heated. 'Shape memory

alloys' can be manipulated when cool, but will revert back to their original state when heated again. They were discovered by William Buehler in 1961.

844 **I**n 1961, George Devol from America designed a robot machine that could weld and paint. Similar designs are still used in car manufacturing today.

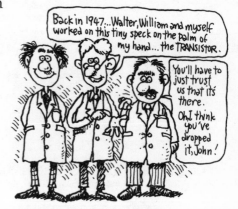

845 **T**he transistor is an essential part of all electronics, as it has the ability to control the electricity inside them. In 1947, the first one was invented by three men, William Shockley, Walter Brattain and John Bardeen.

846 In 1940 Claude Shannon established that the work of 19th century mathematician George Boole could be applied to electronic circuits, providing the foundations of digital logic which all computers rely on.

847 Early computer designs as far back as 1940 were using binary coding thanks to John Atanasoff and Clifford Berry. Binary coding is made up of many 1s and 0s.

848 In 1941, a scientist from Germany called Konrad Zuse made a computer that used mechanical switches rather than electronics.

COMPUTERS IN 1941

Can you have the computer calculate 2 x 10 for me, please?

Sure! Why not leave it with me... pop off...have some lunch perhaps ...a bit of shopping maybe...then nip back and the computer will have the answer for you.

849 The printed circuit board was invented in 1941 by Paul Eisler from Austria. It had the wiring patterns set out in plastic sheets, with holes for wires to be placed in the right positions and places for components to be fitted.

850 The first conductive plastic was invented in 1977 by three scientists, Alan Heeger from America, Hideki Shirakawa from Japan and Alan MacDiarmid from New Zealand.

851 Integrated circuit chips are incredibly important to computers and other electronic equipment. Jack Kilby invented one in 1958 and it contained a few transistors. It was improved upon by Robert Noyce in 1959.

852 FORTRAN is a type of computer coding which is much faster to input than previous forms. It was invented by John Backus in 1957.

853 The first computer to use all electronics rather than mechanics was invented in 1945 by John Propser Eckert and John Mauchley. It was, however, an enormous machine and was superseded later by more practical designs.

854 The memory of a computer is very important, as it is where programs are stored. It is likely that the first computer memory was designed by John von Neumann in Hungary.

855 If it wasn't for the error-correcting code invented by Richard Hamming in 1950, many machines like mobile phones would not work today!

856 The first mini computer was not as 'mini' as we would think of in today's computer age, but it was certainly smaller than the computers that could fill a room. In 1965 Kenneth Olsen from America reduced the size by using the integrated circuit system and it immediately took off around the world.

857 For a long time, computers used a single 'window' or screen for all purposes. In 1968, the graphical user interface (or GUI) was invented by Doug Engelbart. It introduced the concept of different windows for different programs. It was further developed by Alan Kay.

858 The first floppy discs were large 20-centimetre (8-inch) square discs that could contain data. They were invented by the IBM group in 1970. The smaller and decidedly less floppy versions were introduced by Sony in 1980.

859 Ted Hoff was an engineer at the Intel Corporation and he came up with the microprocessor chip in 1971. Without it, we may not have personal computers today.

860 Calculators had been around for some time when, in the 1970s, it was decided to design smaller and more portable models. Various scientists including Jack Kilby, James Van Tassel and Jerry Merryman attempted the pocket calculator. The British inventor Clive Sinclair (later knighted) drew on technology advances for his version, which became vastly popular.

What's the square root of 365 plus 2,400 multiplied by .0058?

Just give me a sec!

IN THE 1970s BEFORE EVERYONE HAD MOBILE PHONES... THEY ALL HAD CALCULATORS.

861 **S**upercomputers can perform tasks that smaller computers are unable to do. The first supercomputer was built by Seymour Cray in 1976 and was given the name 'Cray-1'.

862 **T**here is a fantastic electronic message system called public-key cryptography which involves many different digits of information that can only be deciphered by the person meant to receive them. It was developed in 1977 by a team of scientists and cryptographers.

863 **T**he personal computer was first produced in 1977. Three famous examples are the Tandy®, the Commodore® and the Apple®. The men behind the last, Steve Jobs and Stephen Wozniak, were great promoters and their model took off as the leading computer of the time.

864 **B**ASIC computer code was devised for the beginner of computers. It was written by John Kemeny and Tom Kurtz in 1963.

865 **D**aniel Bricklin and Bob Frankson developed spreadsheet software for computers in 1979. The first program was called VisiCalc® and it revolutionised the use of computers.

866 The IBM personal computer was launched in 1981 by William Lowe and the operating system was supplied by Microsoft, then a fledgling company.

867 The Internet was first considered in 1962 when J. C. R. Licklider thought of networking various computers. In 1969 this was developed into a system called ARPANET. By 1970, new technology made it possible to transfer data from machine to machine. More machines were added to the network and by the 1980s technology allowed the spread of the Internet across the world.

868 The World Wide Web was invented by British physicist Tim Berners-Lee in 1990, when he designed the hypertext software used in web browsers.

869 Until 1993, the World Wide Web was unable to mix text and graphics. Then twenty-one-year-old Marc Andreessen invented 'Mosaic', the first graphical browser, which lead to the development of Netscape and Internet Explorer.

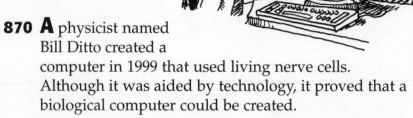

870 A physicist named Bill Ditto created a computer in 1999 that used living nerve cells. Although it was aided by technology, it proved that a biological computer could be created.

871 The Windows® operating system was an invention from the minds at the Microsoft Corporation in 1985.

872 High-temperature superconductors were an invention of for Georg Bednorz and Alex Muller in 1986. Previously, the superconductors used in electromagnets could only work in very low temperatures, so this was an important development.

I just don't like the way that genetically modified flower is looking at me.

873 The first genetically modified flower was the Moondust carnation in 1996, created by the Florigene Limited Company in Australia.

874 The very first cloned animal was the famous Dolly the Sheep. She was the product of genetic engineering by British scientists Ian Wilmut and Keith Campbell in 1996.

875 One of the most important advantages of cloning could be the possibility of helping endangered animals survive. Philip Damiani from Iowa, in the USA, managed to clone the

Well Dolly. You're growing so quickly and you're the spitting image of your Mother, young girl.

Hey... I'm Dolly!

endangered member of the ox family known as the gaur in 2001. The cloned animal, named Noah, gave hope of other animals being saved from extinction.

876 The Omron company in Japan has invented a robotic cat known as NeCoRo. It can copy the movements and habits of a real cat.

877 Numbers have been around for centuries, but the modern numeric system comes from an Arabic form, which was deciphered by Leonardo Pisano in 1202 and used the system of tens and units.

878 The French introduced the metric system in 1789 after the French Revolution, as it was felt to be more practical and logical.

Ahh! Theese new Metreek seestem is...how do you say... confusing. I don't know ten kilo of gurn powder from three metres of rope!

THE NEW METRIC SYSTEM ARRIVED IN FRANCE IN 1789

879 Rockets for space travel were a fantastical dream for many years. There were three men who made the dream into a reality in their own separate professional fields. Robert Goddard (USA), Hermann Oberth (Germany) and Konstantin Eduodovich Tsiolkovsky (Russia) each researched liquid powered rockets in the 1920s.

What does the note say Chen?

It says... You have 10 seconds to big bang!

CHINESE WARFARE 1300s STYLE.

880 Of course, smaller rockets were much simpler and were made by the Chinese following their inventions of gunpowder and fireworks. In approximately 1300, these fireworks were no longer purely for enjoyment, but were employed as weapons when attached to arrows!

881 Space suits were invented out of necessity and were designed by a number of people working for the space program, both in America and Russia. Astronauts needed something to wear

BEFORE SPACE SUITS

that would protect them from pressure in the vacuum of space and from the freezing temperatures.

882 The telescope was invented in 1608 by a Dutch spectacle maker called Hans Lippershey. He noticed that when he looked through two parallel lenses, objects would appear bigger.

883 The Russians launched the first artificial satellite in 1957. It was made by Valentin Glushko and Sergey Korolyuov, and was named Sputnik 1.

884 The first communications satellite, Telstar, was launched in 1962 to relay television signals. However, the first demonstration of a communications satellite took place in 1960 when John Pierce experimented with Echo 1, a satellite balloon that could reflect radio waves.

885 Space flight was a landmark event in humankind's history. Yuri Gagarin from Russia was the very first human being to orbit the Earth, in 1961.

886 The first space station was a team effort from the people at NASA. There was an attempt in 1971 by the Russians, but sadly, it crashed to Earth within half a year. Skylab was NASA's station. It was launched in 1973 and stayed in space until 1979.

887 The space shuttle was another NASA success story. Launched in 1981, it journeyed for fifty-four hours before returning to Earth and landing in a similar way to a plane.

THE SPACE SHUTTLE THINKS IT'S A PLANE.

888 In 1791, Wolfgang von Kempelen invented the very first machine that could produce synthesised sounds. Using the knowledge of human speech as a guide, he created a machine with bellows for artificial lungs and reeds for the thorax, and created a complex system to reproduce sounds mechanically.

889 Auxins are a type of hormone found in plants and are vital for growth but also for making plants reach towards the sun (or other light source). This discovery was made by Friedrich Went in 1926.

Even though it had plenty of auxins in its tissues, the rebellious ivy plant insisted on growing away from the light.

890 The Bunsen burner was not invented by Robert Wilhelm Bunsen, as many believe. It was actually an improved design of Michael Faraday's original concept by Bunsen's lab assistant Peter Desdega, in 1855.

891 The umbrella was originally used as a sun shade. The Chinese and Japanese had lightweight parasols for this purpose. Samuel Fox invented the steel-framed waterproof umbrella in 1874. Not surprisingly, he was from England!

One day when there's a fine sunny day here in England I'll try my newly invented steel-framed umbrella in the sunshine.

The World of Words and Phrases

New words and phrases are invented every day, and work their way into our language. Here are some of the coolest!

892 Affluenza: Someone suffers from this when they spend all their time in the pursuit of purchasing more material objects than they actually need.

893 Anacronym noun: Any acronym where the word has become so entrenched in popular culture that few remember what the letters stand for. For example, RADAR.

894 Beetlemania: A play on words on the term 'Beatlemania', which described the incredible excitement brought on by the Beatles in the 1960s. This new term describes a similar state for those obsessed with Volkswagen Beetles.

Did I show you my super expensive gold neck chain?

Which one?

895 Bling-bling: Describes an abundance of jewellery, particularly on someone who is showing off their money.

896 Bollywood: The world of filmmaking in India.

897 Buns of steel: What you need when forced to sit through something long and boring.

CHARLIE DISCUSSES HIS FUTURE WITH HIS LAWYER.

898 Camouflanguage: Speech that purposefully uses jargon to confuse the listener to hide the real meaning. It is popular with lawyers.

899 Celebreality: A television show about a celebrity's real life.

900 Celebriphilia: When someone is obsessed with a particular celebrity.

901 Chairobics: Exercises for people in wheelchairs.

902 Chick flick: A movie that generally appeals to women rather than men.

903 Chick lit: A book that appeals to women rather than men, and is generally written by a woman too.

904 Chillout: The end of a party when slow-paced music is played and the atmosphere has quietened down.

905 Cyberchondriac: Someone who believes they have a disease because they read about it on the Internet.

906 Dashboard dining: Eating while driving.

907 Dashboard drum: When the dashboard on the car is used for tapping out beats while listening to music.

BY THE THIRD VERSE OF HIS STEERING WHEEL DRUM SOLO, AL HAD MANAGED TO BLOCK 200 CARS WITH FOUR CHANGES OF TRAFFIC LIGHTS AND WENT ON TO FINISH THE TRACK, BLOCKING 1500 CARS.

908 Delhi belly: You may get this if you have eaten a strong curry!

909 Denglish: A mixture of English and German words.

910 Dictionary flame: A message that nit-picks all the grammatical and spelling errors in your work.

911 Eater-tainment: Describes restaurants that are themed in such a way as to provide entertainment while you eat.

912 Ego wall: A wall in someone's home that displays many certificates and awards.

Marilyn was promised a night out with a difference and that's what she got at the BIG TEXAS SPARE RIB LINE DANCING THEATRE RESTAURANT.

913 Email fatigue: This occurs when you have spent a long time going through all the emails you have received in one day, or when you have come back from holiday and found hundreds!

914 Facebase: A database of faces. Often used by the police force when trying to find a criminal.

915 Falloween: The period of time surrounding Halloween in which various parties take place and decorations are displayed.

916 **F**anfic: New stories about television shows and characters written by the fans for their own amusement.

917 **G**iraffiti: Graffiti that is written in impossibly high places.

918 **G**lobesity: The worldwide problem of obesity, especially in the western world.

919 **G**oogle: To search for information on the Internet – often by using the Google search engine.

920 **G**roundhog day: An event that repeats over and over again. Taken from the movie of the same name.

921 **H**ammock: Used to describe screening a less popular television program between two higher-rated programs in order to get better viewing figures.

922 Hyperdating: The desperate act of dating as many people as possible in a short space of time.

923 Idea hamster:
A creative person who just keeps on coming up with new ideas.

924 Internot: To describe someone who absolutely won't use the Internet.

925 IT rage: You may get this when you get frustrated with technology and it just won't do what you want it to do!

926 Japanimation: Animation from Japan, specifically anime.

927 Jargonaut: A person who uses far too much jargon.

928 Juggle eggs: Used to describe performing a difficult mental problem without breaking concentration.

929 Jump the shark: The point in a television show when you know the producers are struggling to keep the series fresh by introducing something totally unexpected. This usually indicates the beginning of the end!

930 Jurassic Park syndrome: You have this if you believe extinct animals can be brought back to life through cloning.

931 Keyboard plaque: The gunk that builds up in between the keys of your computer keyboard.

932 Kiddydrome: A large shop specialising in products for children.

933 Killer litter: Waste products thrown from tall buildings.

934 Kneemail: A prayer said when you are kneeling down.

935 Knowbie: Someone who is a prolific user of the Internet and is very knowledgeable about it.

936 Lad mag: A magazine dedicated to the stuff that interests men more than women.

937 Life coach: Someone who acts as a guide for someone else to help him or her find the right path in life.

938 Liposculpture: The practice of transforming your looks through surgery.

939 Logophilia: Where you have a passion for vocabulary.

940 Lottery mentality: You have this if you believe a sudden windfall of money will solve all your problems.

941 Marmalade-dropper: A shocking headline that you might read in the newspaper over breakfast.

942 Mathlete: Someone who performs in mathematical competitions.

943 Meatloaf: An email containing a joke or a chain letter that has been forwarded by one person to many others.

944 Me-moir: A rather self-obsessed autobiography.

945 Metrosexual: Describes a male who is obsessed with his personal grooming and lifestyle.

946 Mouse potato: Someone who spends most of his or her free time on the computer.

947 Mythic arc: The story within a television series that spreads over more than one episode.

948 Nailing jelly to a tree: To describe a messy and difficult problem.

949 Newbie: Someone who is new to something like a job or the Internet, and often gets things wrong through lack of knowledge.

The carrying the jelly into the yard and finding a tree part of nailing jelly to a tree was fine ... Picking up the hammer was ok too ... But Arnold ran into problems when he actually tried nailing the jelly to the tree.

It's actually a bit harder than it looks!

950 Nintendo thumb: What you get when you play computer games for far too long.

I think the best cure for those thumbs, young man, is no computer games for two weeks... plenty of schoolwork ...plenty of homework ... and lots of playing outside!

951 Numeronymous: Used to describe the telephone numbers on television where the numbers spell out words. For example, 1800 FREE PIES.

952 One-banana problem: An easy problem that won't take long to solve.

953 Oprahisation: When celebrities discuss their personal problems in public arenas; from the TV host Oprah Winfrey.

954 Outernet: Any form of media predating the Internet, newspapers, television, radio, etc.

955 Paparazzification: The process of 'dumbing-down' to make something easier to understand when it often isn't necessary.

956 Paraskevidekatriaphobia: You would have this if you were terrified of Friday the thirteenth (the date, not the movie!).

957 Peeping-Tom TV: Describes television shows that focus on real people doing real life stuff; also known as reality TV.

958 Pink-slip party: A gathering to console someone who has just lost their job.

959 Poop fiction: Books that use toilet humour to appeal to kids.

960 Privatopia: A gated community in which all the inhabitants abide by certain rules.

961 Pygmalionism: When you are obsessed with something you have created yourself.

962 Quarterlife crisis: When someone in their mid-twenties panics about their future.

963 Quirkyalone: Someone who is happier to live alone than seek a partner.

964 Reset generation: People who repeatedly get bored with a situation quickly, give up and start something new.

965 ROM brain: Someone who can't accept ideas from other people.

966 Rumourtism: You may have this if you spread rumours with conviction as if they were facts.

967 Rush minute: Similar to the rush hour before and immediately after work, only shorter if you live close by.

968 Salad dodger: Someone who prefers to eat unhealthy food.

969 Screenager: A young person who has grown up learning about life through television and computers.

970 Screwball noir: A movie combining screwball comedy and the aspects of film noir.

971 Severely gifted: A very bright and intelligent child.

972 Sleep camel: Someone who gets very little sleep during the week and then sleeps all weekend.

973 Snaparazzi: Photographers who take pictures of famous people and sell them to the press.

974 Spam: Unwanted emails that fill up your inbox.

975 Stress puppy: Someone who enjoys complaining about the stress they are under.

976 Swarm logic: When a large group of unintelligent creatures work together to make thing work.

The 258,324 killer bees from the hive work together to chase Barry from the forest... in fact, into the next state!

977 Talking hairdo: A television presenter who is employed mainly for their looks and cares more about self-presentation than the topic being discussed.

978 TEOTWAWKI: This is an acronym that stands for The End Of The World As We Know It.

979 Testosteronic: Said of guys who overtly display their masculinity.

980 Toxic bachelor: A single guy who is so afraid of commitment that he comes across as offensive.

981 Transwestite: Someone who likes to dress like a cowboy, even though they aren't one.

982 T-shirt-able: A slogan or catchphrase that has the appeal of being printed on a T-shirt. For example, 'Eat my shorts'.

983 Undecorating: To redecorate in a way that tones down a room to make it simpler.

984 Undertime: Time off from work to do personal stuff.

985 Uninstalled: When 'been sacked' seems too harsh to say.

986 Urban forest: A small area of trees and wildlife within a city.

987 Vacation hangover: That horrible feeling the first week back at school or work after a rather enjoyable holiday.

988 Vampire time: Time spent going out late at night and spending the daylight hours sleeping it off.

989 Voken: The small icon on a web page that is linked to an advertisement pop-up window.

990 Voyear: Someone who eavesdrops frequently.

991 Vulcan nerve pinch: Taken from the television series 'Star Trek' (where a pinch to the neck would supposedly render someone unconscious), this refers to using 'ctrl, alt, del' on the computer when in a sticky situation.

992 Watercooler effect: Often said of television programs that get discussed and promoted through word of mouth during coffee breaks in the workplace.

993 Weblish: The grammatically incorrect and badly punctuated language often posted Web-based forums, emails and public reviews in online stores.

994 Wordrobe: A person's vocabulary.

995 Work rage: A symptom of frustration within the workplace.

996 Xenotransplant: Implanting animal organs into humans.

997 Yell phone: A mobile phone into which someone is speaking very loudly.

998 Yuck factor: Said of something if it contains something displeasing or horrible.

999 Zen mail: A blank email.

1000 Zitcom: A situation comedy starring and aimed at teenagers.

1001 Zorse: A cross between a zebra and a horse.